The Divinity of Dogs

ALSO BY JENNIFER SKIFF

God Stories

The
DIVINITY
of DOGS

*True Stories of Miracles Inspired
by Man's Best Friend*

Jennifer Skiff

ATRIA BOOKS

NEW YORK   LONDON   TORONTO   SYDNEY   NEW DELHI

ATRIA BOOKS

A Division of Simon & Schuster, Inc.
1230 Avenue of the Americas
New York, NY 10020

First Atria Books hardcover edition October 2012

ATRIA BOOKS and colophon are trademarks of Simon & Schuster, Inc.

For information about special discounts for bulk purchases,
please contact Simon & Schuster Special Sales at 1-866-506-1949 or
business@simonandschuster.com.

The Simon & Schuster Speakers Bureau can bring authors to your live event. For more information or to book an event, contact the Simon & Schuster Speakers Bureau at 1-866-248-3049 or visit our website at www.simonspeakers.com.

Designed by Dana Sloan

Manufactured in the United States of America

10 9 8 7 6 5 4 3 2 1

Library of Congress Cataloging-in-Publication Data is available.

ISBN 978-1-4516-2157-0
ISBN 978-1-4516-2160-0 (ebook)

For Jon,
CousCous, and ChickPea
my happy family

For engulfing me in a warm
blanket of love for sixteen years
and for teaching me about
joy, courage, and humanity

I could not love you more.

Contents

Introduction

Divine (di·vine) 1. Relating to or being directly from God 2. Having godlike nature 3. Lovely

This was a difficult book to write. It's a memoir and a book of other people's experiences. Documenting the trials of people and how dogs have helped them through those trials has been a privilege. But reliving my own difficulties was humbling, at times disturbing, and often sad as I forced myself to remember the times so many beautiful souls have helped me through the challenges of my life. I've shed many tears while writing this book.

I believe life is a journey and that we're here to learn and grow spiritually. I also believe dogs are a gift from the Divine sent here to help us on our way. *The Divinity of Dogs* is about people's moments of enlightenment with dogs. It includes stories in which love, tolerance, comfort, compassion, loyalty, joyfulness, and even death have provided inspirational lessons about life from experiences with dogs.

Whether you believe dogs are divine or a gift from the Divine, *The Divinity of Dogs* gives you permission to accept what you know: dogs provide us with a clear example of all that is good. They are healers, educators, protectors, and tangible examples of divine love. For those of you who agree with this philosophy, this book confirms all we know and puts an exclamation point on it!

It wasn't until I edited my first book, *God Stories,* and received thousands of stories about people's connection with the Divine, that I realized my personal experience with dogs was shared with countless others. People wrote and told me about the private moments that changed their lives. Their stories were profound and amazing—the type that warm your heart and make you cry out loud. They catapulted me into other people's trials, leaving me with a sense of appreciation for all I have. I decided these were stories that needed to be told, to document the divinity of dogs and to give us a library of inspiring life lessons. Writing *The Divinity of Dogs,* for me, was also very personal.

My dogs have gently guided me through life. As a child, when I was fearful and sad, my Golden Retriever, Sally, was my strength and savior. Later in life, when I was recovering from a tumor in my bone marrow, Philophal, a mix of Terrier and Poodle, and Nicky, a Basenji-Lab cross, would jump on me until I got out of bed each day. Nicky's separation anxiety, and the destructive behavior that came with it, gave me a lesson in patience, while Mary the Spitz calmed my storms and taught me how to love. Clara the Boxer was my first friend, and Clemmie the Cockapoo my first rescue. Chickpea, my one-eyed Shih Tzu, has been the child I never had, while CousCous the Maltese-Pomeranian has licked me awake with love and questionable breath every morning. When at times I didn't want to go on any longer, my love for dogs kept me here.

My dogs have been the reason I have woken up every single day of my life with a smile on my face. They have protected me from mean people and have given me insight into potential partners. They have been my children and my parents. They have loved me the most. I am among the ranks of millions of people who appreciate the souls of dogs and know they are a gift of pure love and an example of all that is good. More than anything, they have taught me how to be a better person. I'm not alone. The world is filled with people who have reached the same conclusion and are happy to share why.

- Scott Thornsley thought his life was over. He lost his job of nineteen years, and his wife left him. He felt no one loved or wanted him. He decided to kill himself. At the very moment he chose to act on his decision, his Rottweiler, Emma, ran into the room, grabbed his hand ferociously, and pulled him to the front door. What happened next, in the darkest moment of his life, saved him.
- Joy Peterkin lost her home and belongings in Hurricane Katrina—but she still had her Chihuahua, Little Bit. Just as Joy was finding some normalcy in her life, Little Bit began persistently nudging a spot on her breast. In this book, we find out what Little Bit knew that doctors didn't.
- Mazie the Lab was on death row at a shelter. She was rescued by a prison canine-training program and then by a service-dog charity. Freda Powell was in her own battle with life. She was a deaf parent with autistic twin boys and was trying to survive the loss of her oldest son in a heartbreaking tragedy. The last thing Freda wanted was a dog, until Mazie came and rescued her entire family.
- Alyssa Denis was in her early twenties when she was diagnosed with severe systemic lupus. She was a shut-in, confined to her bed, in pain and living alone. Doctors told her she wouldn't live past the age of twenty-five. That's when she applied for a service

dog. In this book, you learn how Luna the Labrador gave Alyssa a reason to get up and live the life she was told she'd never have.

• In 1956 and 1957, a number of teenagers in Chicago were brutally murdered by a suspected serial killer. Gloria Wardrum was nineteen and worked during the day. The only time she could walk her always-friendly Airedale Terrier, Ginger, was in the evening. One afternoon, at dusk, while playing with Ginger in a park, Gloria fell asleep against a tree. She abruptly awoke to Ginger's fierce growls as the dog tugged at her leash, trying to get to a man who was approaching. The man was twisting a rope between his hands as he got closer. What happened next proved to Gloria the divinity of dogs.

Miracles associated with dogs have been documented throughout history and are one of the reasons people have always felt a heavenly connection to them. Thousands of years ago, in Mesopotamia, a land that is now Iraq, followers of Gula, the Goddess of Healing, actually called the dog "The Divinity." Egyptians had dog-gods and were often buried with dogs to guide and protect them in the afterlife. Aboriginal people on every continent have connected dogs to holy places. Tribes, religions, and societies throughout time have considered the dog a god. What's amazing is that before there were easy means of long-distance communication, people in separate parts of the world felt the same way about dogs.

Jesus Christ, one of the most influential people in history, asked people to strive for certain character qualities for which dogs are well known: joyfulness, generosity, love, sensitivity, compassion, tolerance, contentment, forgiveness, loyalty, patience, gratefulness, enthusiasm, and dependability. Who do you know in your house who possesses these qualities at all times? In my house (it's hard to admit, but it's true), the only selfless love comes from the dogs. Recently, torn between being with my husband in Australia and rushing to the side of my dying dog CousCous in the United States, things got heated. I turned to my husband and said, "I love her more than I love you. She's my baby. Your love has conditions. Hers doesn't." He smiled and then laughed. What a great guy! I got on the next plane. CousCous lived!

How can a dog possess all the character traits we strive for but can never completely achieve? Are their dispositions divine, or are dogs actually gifts from the Divine? The stories in this book provide some of the answers to those questions.

Today, published medical research confirms that people with dogs have reduced stress, lower blood pressure, less heart disease, and they suffer from lower rates of depression than people who don't have dogs. These days, we have therapy dogs who visit hospitals and nursing homes, guide dogs who protect, sniffer dogs who rescue, police dogs who serve, and dogs who doctors agree can reach a sick child when medicine and other people can't.

I am a person who has received the gift of emotional healing from a dog. When I was seven years old, a Retriever named Sally was my best friend, confidante, and constant companion. She enthusiastically watched as I danced and sang along to David Cassidy records and rejoiced in our walks along the rocky coastline of Maine. We lived a happy life. A few years later, my parents' marriage ended, and I moved into a house with a cruel and inhumane stepfather. My world rocked as I became a victim and lived a fearful existence. My only constant was Sally. I was no longer permitted to sleep with her, but when I could, I'd sneak outdoors to the kennel and lie with her on the concrete, the only place where all was warm, loving, and safe.

Many people share similar stories. The solace we get from dogs is like a warm blanket of love engulfing us, no matter our worries. This book is a glimpse into the lives of people who have been inspired by a dog.

Many of the dogs in this book are rescues. That means they were given up, abandoned, confiscated for cruelty, or lost and ended up at a shelter. Many were scheduled to die and were rescued at the last minute. I have asked the contributors to this book to nominate a charity at the end of each story, to give you the chance to see the good work being done by people throughout the world, to help the voiceless. Most of the dogs in this book came from the charities in their stories. If you allow yourself to become immersed in each story and its message, I promise you the clouds in your own sky will dissipate as you realize all you have and how simple it is to live your life joyfully.

As much as we look up at the stars and know there is more than life on earth, the divinity of dogs is just as unexplainable and profound. They may be the purest example of divine love in an earthly soul many of us ever experience. If we take their lead, open our hearts, and embrace their love, we may just find our own journey a lot more enlightening.

Love

Embracing the Gift

Bookie and Jennifer

Shortly after I began searching for stories for this book, I received an e-mail from the director of the Israeli Guide Dog Center for the Blind. He asked me if I knew the Hebrew name for dog and what it meant. I did not. The name, he said, is *Kel-lev*, and means "full of heart."

Talk about a revelation. It was as if someone had handed me the lost key to my personal safe, the place where I held my opinions about dogs locked up, for fear of being criticized for them.

This ancient translation suggested to me that people understood the gift of dogs more than three thousand years ago. Many millions of people before us had acknowledged that a dog is full of heart, the organ that sustains us and is associated with love.

For me, the knowledge started at birth with a Boxer named Clara, whom I called Bookie. I am the eldest of six children, and for the first two years of my life, I was an only child. But I wasn't alone. Many of my baby pictures show the head of a chubby infant attached to the cheek of a tan-colored Boxer with pointed ears and a black snout.

I can't tell you much about my life with Bookie other than that we were inseparable, and when I was seven, she died. What I can tell you with certainty is that I've always missed her.

Thirty-three years after she passed, my father walked into my kitchen for his morning coffee, waving a video. He said he'd found an old reel of black-and-white film in the attic and had converted it to tape for my fortieth birthday.

As I sat down with him, I could barely contain my excitement. My parents had been divorced for nearly thirty years. I remembered little of my early childhood in Hyannis, Massachusetts. My mother's recollections of her life with my father had left me disheartened. She had given me the impression that, for her, it had been "time" to get married and that there had been little love in their years together.

I turned on the video, and as I watched, tears welled in my eyes. It was winter. There were two young people having a snowball fight. They were playful and affectionate. There was a lot of laughter. There was a baby, bundled in blankets, nestled in a silver Flexible Flyer snow saucer. The baby was pushed down a snow bank, and her dog ran alongside.

The seasons changed, and it was summer. There was a picnic by the ocean. The child was now sitting up. She was on a blanket with her dog, and they were leaning against each other, both smiling. Someone threw the dog a stick, and she chased it, plunging into the water, grabbing it in her mouth, and bringing it back to the child, causing a series of excited giggles. The two parents were clearly delighted with their accomplishment and each other.

There had been love after all—a lot of it. My parents had adored each other and me. I had also known the divinity of a dog whose pure love had come without conditions and had been carried in my heart throughout my life. Bookie had instilled in me an important lesson: love between people often changes and ends, but you can always count on the unwavering love of a dog.

Bookie marked the beginning of my journey with dogs.

"I had no reason to live"

Scott Thornsley

It was Christmas morning, 1995. My wife had left me in August, and two weeks later, I lost my job of nineteen years. I was alone, without anyone to turn to. Worst of all, no one needed me anymore—my workplace or the wife I loved.

I'd just gotten my PhD and was looking forward to enjoying the success that would come with it. Instead, the hunt for a new job was futile. Because of my new degree, I couldn't get the most menial of jobs. Most people said I was overeducated. I felt like a total failure.

I thought long and hard and came to the conclusion that my life was not worth living. I decided to commit suicide.

The moment came. I'd decided on a method and was committed to carrying it out. At that very moment, my four-year-old Rottweiler, Emma, bounded into the study. Her leash was in her mouth, which was not unusual. What was unusual was what she did next. She grabbed my hand with her mouth and ferociously pulled me toward the front door, tugging and yanking me out of my chair. She had never done this before.

There was a hard-falling snow, which would make even the

shortest of walks difficult. Her tugging continued. I decided to grant her one more walk.

Once we were outside, she wouldn't let me go home. She continued, just ahead, leading me through neighborhoods and school athletic fields. Emma wandered without direction, refusing to let me turn around. A couple of hours passed, and during that time, my mind cleared, and I realized my life was not over. I had much to be thankful for, and someone really did need me—even if it was a female Rottweiler named Emma. There is no doubt in my mind that Emma saved my life that day.

In the darkest of moments, a dog can make your life worth living.

Emma & Scott

North East Rottweiler Rescue & Referral
rottrescue.org

"The secret magic entrusted to dogs"

Camille Boisvert

The ability to love may be easily extinguished by the harshness of the world. Like overused elastic, a hardened heart seems impossible to flex and reshape ever again. No gesture of kindness or promise of sincerity can be trusted by an injured soul. People around the world make their way each day through all that life brings—good, bad, and terribly bad—with a knowing attitude of defeat. Many do not know about the secret magic entrusted to dogs.

This is the story of Molly B, a chocolate Labrador Retriever with golden eyes, and me, when I was a thirty-nine-year-old woman with a closed heart.

We were brought together one snowy white day just before Christmas in 1994. As a gift to my life partner, Denise, we drove to a breeder and bought the plumpest, squiggliest Lab pup in the litter. Denise already knew the secret about dogs, which is learned by experience, and always had at least one dog in her life. I, on the other hand, didn't know much about dogs and, to be truthful, was easily irritated by them. I went along with having dogs to keep Denise happy because I loved her.

Love can be divided into two categories: guarded and unguarded. Guarded love keeps you safe so that only small amounts of pain and disappointment can leak into your heart and soul. It is sensible and responsible. Unguarded love is risky and can bring unbearable pain.

Molly cried enough the first night that we gave in and let her sleep on the bed with us. A few nights later, we woke to a strange moaning. Molly's jaw was clenched, and her legs and claws were extended. Her body was rigid.

The doctor told us Molly was epileptic and would have periodic seizures for the rest of her life. He said that someday, Molly would have to take daily medicine to control the seizures, but for the first year or so, she could live without medication. He told us we would have to watch Molly carefully to prevent her from falling down stairs or receiving other injuries during a seizure. This was when I started to sincerely care about the welfare of our dog.

Every morning, I'd read the newspaper and drink hot coffee for thirty minutes in the sunroom before starting my day. One morning, Molly came and lay next to me with her nose on my feet. She didn't move until I got up. It was adorable and made me feel special, but I didn't think much of it otherwise. The next day, Molly did the same thing, and then every day after that.

To my surprise, Denise told me that Molly had bonded with me. Somehow this little pup had gotten close to me without me being able to control it. It made me feel important and necessary to the life of the little Lab, and I felt responsible for keeping her safe and happy. More and more, I wanted to look after Molly and protect her from danger and keep her happy by playing ball and taking walks. The bond between us grew stronger every day, which made me hesitate occasionally. But the love I was feeling for Molly was too great to stop.

Each and every little curiosity in life was a novelty to Molly. There was incredible joy in witnessing her growth and development. Her seizures continued, and I was always quick to take over the care of our sick little dog. The more seizures Molly had, the more guarding I was over her welfare, instead of being guarded in the amount of love I let in or out.

We were hopeful the seizures would remain minor and we wouldn't have to medicate Molly. But one night when Molly was an adult, she had a seizure that wouldn't stop. We had to carry her into the truck and drive her to the emergency clinic. All the while, Molly remained rigid, grunting and moaning, with her claws extended. The doctor administered a Valium drip, and the seizure went away. But that night, everything changed.

There are large and small dramas that play out in the lives of us all every day. Sometimes we take them in stride, and sometimes we fall down. It's a time to think about what's really happening and to remember that our reaction usually affects the people, or in this case the dog, around us. I was inclined to think only about how the world was affecting me and would forget about the people around me. The dramas would become inflated, and sometimes I'd act irrationally. But this was different. All I cared about was Molly's health.

The doctor said Molly would have to take phenobarbital every day for the rest of her life and that it would eventually result in liver failure. It would be unavoidable and final.

The next morning, we began putting the pill in Molly's food. It became routine and was a daily reminder that Molly would have a short life. There were more seizures but nothing life-threatening. I kept Molly from harm whenever possible and realized that as I cared for her, I felt unconditional love. It was a new and foreign feeling to me, one that needed consideration. Believe it or not, I actually took the time to decide to allow myself to give unconditional love and to receive it from this eighty-pound, bounding, bouncing network of muscle, fur, and teeth. Why? Why on earth would "just a dog" be the one to allow me to finally release this unreasonable fear of loving? The reason is that it was not possible for Molly to give conditional love. The more love I gave my dog, the more love I got back. It was as simple as that.

Eventually, after ten great years of living with us, Molly became sick from the medicine. There were several episodes of running to the emergency room, and then one day I saw that Molly's brown tail was turning yellow. I knew it was time. It was the most gut-wrenching moment of my life, making the decision to let her go. To drive Molly to the vet's office, witness the administering of the euthanasia, and hold her while she passed away was like throwing innocence off a cliff because God said it must be done.

When I got home after leaving Molly to be cremated, I took a walk by myself in the woods. The taking of life in any form was unacceptable to me. This process of letting go of a beloved pet was such a violation to my own philosophy that I felt transported to some alternative universe where love and loss were vines that intertwined and wound around inside my every bone and vein. The vines pulled tighter and tighter, and my breathing became staggered as tears flooded down my cheeks and onto my clothes. A force welled up from my gut and came screaming out of my mouth. An unsolicited moaning scream came out, and I held it until I couldn't breathe. Then I sat down and just cried my heart out. It was a manifestation of grief, the monster that I feared before I'd learned to love.

There in the woods, I looked at grief, and I looked at love—the intertwined vines of life. I thought about life without Molly, life without unconditional love, and made a decision. Molly's legacy for me would be to live my life with the courage to love.

The secret magic entrusted to dogs is that they will show you how to love. All you have to do is give them unconditional love. If you can do that, you will learn to love the world around you—and you must not care if it loves you back. Just know that if a waterfall of love pours from you, all creatures that pass through will pause to take in the moment, however brief, of relief from the harshness of the world.

Molly B

Best Friends Animal Society
bestfriends.org

Cooper

Roxy Reading Therapy Dogs
roxyreading.org

"My husband and I were never able to have children"

Connie Bandy

My husband and I were never able to have children. After in vitro fertilization, two miscarriages, and an adoption that fell through, we decided it wasn't meant to be. So we got a little Shih Tzu dog named Cooper until we could figure out what our next step would be.

Cooper was a blessing! Being naturally cute and fluffy, he immediately formed bonds with the children in our neighborhood. He became such a hit that kids would come over and knock on the door to see if Cooper could play with them. After he received the title of "neighborhood dog," I realized Cooper had a unique ability to bond with children.

I enrolled Cooper in several obedience programs, and he became certified as a therapy dog. It was through the therapy dog classes that I was introduced to a woman named Diane Smith and her reading program called Roxy Reading. Diane started the program after she discovered that children's reading skills improved significantly when they read aloud to her dog, Roxy. Teachers applauded the program when they saw its effects, noting significant improvement with the kids right off the bat. Introverted and shy children suddenly perked up when they read to Roxy. When I heard about the program, I instantly knew it was where Cooper and I belonged.

My "aha" moment happened after a Roxy Reading session. I had been very angry and depressed about not being able to conceive. We had been visiting a third-grade class of seven- and eight-year-olds. The kids were sitting in a circle and, one by one, took turns reading to Cooper. The child who was reading was able to stroke and get kisses from Cooper as he read. I noticed the kids were getting more proficient with their reading skills since working with Cooper. I loved seeing the progress, the kids loved the reading, and Cooper loved being there.

After the session, I got back into the car with Cooper and was feeling pretty good about the hour. I thought back on how he had made everyone laugh and how much pleasure he brought the children. I looked over at him, sitting in the passenger seat, and was filled with an incredible sense of joy and love for my little dog.

At that moment, I realized I didn't have to have my own child to make a difference in a child's life. Together, Cooper and I were making a difference in young people's lives. We were helping them learn to read and were encouraging a lifelong love of reading.

I'm at peace now. Cooper truly is an angel in the form of a dog. Because of him, I'm surrounded by children all the time.

God works in mysterious ways. Through Cooper, I've come to learn that disappointments make way for other areas of love and growth to come into our lives.

"Oh, yes, you loved him"

Jeremy Ashton

In my mid-forties, I was feeling the hitherto unfelt, painful emotions of a lost childhood and felt compelled to travel back to England, where I'd lived until the age of ten. I feared no happy memories awaited my pilgrimage. I felt particularly drawn to visit the old farmhouse where circumstances had forced my family to live during World War II

My father had been a conscientious objector who refused to participate in the war. He and my mother were both artists, hippies of that era, with progressive and alternative concepts long before they were popular. My father was a political rebel. Since he wouldn't go to war, British law forced him to work on a farm for minimal pay.

Just after I was born and the war was ending, my father left England for a job in Africa, where he died in a horrible accident.

My mother was left alone with three children. Life became very difficult. My older brother took his anger out on me. My mother, who already had difficulty with emotional warmth, became even more distant. She decided to give me up. For several years, I lived happily with a German couple who loved me until my mother came back and forced my return to her. By then, she was remarried into a family with terrible problems. There was evil there. And there was abuse.

Decades had now passed, and I traveled back to the farmhouse in Salcott, Essex. Amazingly, the doctor who currently lived there was accommodating. "Take all the time you want; look inside, wander the grounds," he said. The interior caught my earliest memories. It was real, and it was dark.

I walked outside and took in the scenery. The farmhouse is in an unusual location, where the flat Essex land almost enters the sea, with earth dykes like in Holland. Here I could breathe, and I walked around with the doctor's little dog leading. He was one of those small, happy breeds we want to call "doggies" rather than dogs. He led me to the old sea wall, the place we had called "the dyke." He showed me the view. I watched as he sniffed the sweet sea air with me. He showed me that, yes, there had been some light and life even in that sad childhood.

A few days later, I was in another region of England, visiting my German parents, Elizabeth and Walter. I told them about my trip to the farmhouse, and we began to reminisce. They'd been there and had known my parents. Elizabeth spoke of the farmhouse as she remembered it and then said, "And there was your dear little doggie."

I interrupted. "I don't remember any dog."

"Oh, yes, you loved him a lot. You called him Shrimp and used to follow him around the place."

And then she described Shrimp. If it wasn't the same dog I'd met a few days before, it was close enough to undo me inside. In a way beyond words, I understood someone had been there for me during one of my darkest times.

When I think of Shrimp now, I sense the inexplicable help present in the midst of impossible times. Today I can call this God, but in those times, it was nothing I could name. Shrimp was proof that God was there for me in my early childhood, along with the daylight, the fresh air, and the sea.

My life changed after this experience. I became open to the many ways God can be present so that emotional healing can occur.

The Humane Society of the United States
humanesociety.org

"I was no longer alone"

Amy Browne

After a lonely year following a divorce, I embarked on a cross-country road trip with two friends. We were traveling from Maine to Idaho, where we would join environmentalists who were gathering to oppose the commercial logging of one of the largest roadless tracts of land left in the United States. When we got there, we'd be camping for a week in the mountains. Along the way, we'd be sleeping where we could.

On the morning after Midsummer's Night, we pulled into a highway rest area near Delphos, Ohio. In the parking area, a tiny apricot-colored Poodle was running alongside the semi-trailer trucks as they pulled away. It was an accident waiting to happen. One of my friends caught the dog and began a search for his owner. He walked among the cars in the parking lot, trying to find the car or truck he'd escaped from. But no one claimed him. He didn't have a collar. The staff in the rest area office said they could call animal rescue but couldn't keep him safely in the office. They also said they didn't know if anyone would respond to their call. We had a dilemma. So we left our phone number along with a

Amy and Puck

Bangor Humane Society
bangorhumane.org

note that said, "We're bringing your dog to Idaho. We'll be back in a week."

We named the dog Puck after the clever and mischievous elf-like creature in the Shakespeare play *A Midsummer Night's Dream.* He quickly lived up to his name. Once we hit the mountains of Idaho, he became the "wilderness Poodle." He spent the first few days staring down rattlesnakes, surviving a hike in the desert that turned out to be much longer than expected, braving severe thunderstorms in the Badlands, and fearlessly crossing log bridges high above raging rapids. The more sticks and sage he caught in his hair, the happier he seemed. We bought him dog food, but he preferred to eat what we did, which included a lot of pan-fried bread.

One night in the Rocky Mountains, I realized how devoted my new friend was. I was sleeping under the stars, at a distance from other campers. Puck stayed awake all night standing guard. A few times, he growled and snarled, seeming to chase off the unknown creatures of the night. The little guy was willing to put his fifteen-pound body on the line to protect me. It was then I realized I'd do the same for him.

No one ever came looking for Puck in Ohio. Our new friend stayed with us as we crossed the country.

When we reached Maine, I dropped off my last passenger, and a sinking feeling hit me as I prepared to drive back to my empty house. And then I looked at the seat next to me and realized I was no longer alone.

I'd finally been open to receiving again, and what I needed was magically provided. I had devotion in the form of a Poodle who loved the wilderness and me.

"A heart of love"

Renee Gutzmann

My husband, Fred, and I were in Baja, Mexico, staying in a little hut-style bungalow, when we were awoken at 3 A.M. by a strange thumping at the door. I was very nervous. We had been warned about thieves in the area. Fred cautiously opened the door, and at his feet was a dog, wagging his tail. Fred closed the door, and the thumping started again.

After a brief discussion, we opened the door and invited the dog in. He was tan-colored, with a long tail and dark eyes. He was also very bony.

We went to the fridge and pulled out some leftovers and gave them to him. After he ate, he did the strangest thing; he actually smiled. He then licked us both, leaned against us, and walked out the open door with his tail wagging.

The next morning, we left some clothes on the beach and took a rubber dinghy to a nearby reef to snorkel. As we looked back at the beach, we noticed that the same dog from the early-morning visit was sitting by our stuff. When we returned two hours later, he was still there.

As we came out of the water, his tail began to wag, and he started nosing something in the sand, showing it to me. I looked down and saw that it was a rock, a perfectly shaped, white, polished, heart-shaped rock.

The moment was mysteriously wonderful. The dog looked up at Fred and me standing there with our mouths open. It was as if something divine was happening. "How could he have done that? How did he get that rock?" Fred questioned. I didn't have the answer. I picked up the rock, and after lots of kisses and petting, the dog took off down the beach. We never saw him again.

The dog gave us a gift, a heart of love, in response to a simple kindness. He loved us and was grateful for us. I learned from that rare, found friend to love everything and everyone without a reason.

Companion Animal Placement Assistance

lompoccapa.com

"She was totally submerged"

Jeanne Bowen

After watching days of horrific news coverage following Hurricane Katrina, I decided to volunteer with the Humane Society of the United States crisis team. My assignment was a temporary animal shelter in Hattiesburg, Mississippi. The first dog I saw was the saddest, skinniest, most unresponsive dog I'd ever seen. She was a large dog, a tricolored Treeing Walker Coonhound. I felt a huge sense of empathy for her and cried, unable to imagine what her sweet soul must have endured. I knew at that moment that she could have a beautiful life with my family, and I named her Bella, for beautiful.

After several months passed and her owners were never found, I brought Bella home and introduced her to Cricket, my red-and-tan-colored Welsh Corgi. Bella knew she had come into Cricket's home and went with the flow. Cricket took a while to adjust to the intruder.

Despite Cricket's hesitation, Bella instantly became Cricket's protector. One night, while I was walking the dogs in the woods, a bobcat appeared out of nowhere and tried to take Cricket. Bella lunged at the bobcat, forcing it to retreat and run.

A year later, Cricket fell from a grooming table. Her spinal cord was severed, and she was paralyzed. We had her fitted for a wheel cart, and as she learned to live with the drastic change in her life, Bella stepped up to protect her even more. She was a serene and accepting dog and always looked after Cricket lovingly.

In March 2010, Bella passed away. Cricket went into a deep depression.

Six months passed. It was a beautiful summer day, and I decided to do some gardening. The yard has a spring-fed pond, a lupine meadow, and stone gardens that overlook the sea. Lots of birds and other animals congregate around the pond, and Cricket loves to explore that area searching for frogs. While I gardened, Cricket was watching the wildlife in her cart near the pond.

Every now and then, I'd look up and check on her. She was always in the same spot, a few feet from the water. I continued gardening, making a quick trip to the compost heap on the side of the house. I came back and assumed that Cricket was where I had last seen her. Several minutes later, I went to bring her inside but couldn't see her on the grass. I called her name. No response. I ran to the pond and looked in. She was totally submerged in the water and wasn't moving.

I grabbed the back of the cart and pulled her out, upside down, and shook her. I could tell she was alive because her eyes looked at me, but she wasn't moving. I rushed her into the house and put her into a hot bath. When she did start to move, it was clear she was hypothermic, because she couldn't stop shaking. After the bath, as I was drying her with the hair dryer, she kept looking up over her right shoulder. I actually told her no one was there, but she kept looking over her shoulder at something. Through the night, she kept lifting herself up with her two front legs, looking at something I couldn't see.

The next morning, as I was walking through the house, I saw a quick movement outside the window. It was like a blur of quick-moving energy. At that moment, I knew it was Bella and that her spirit had saved Cricket from drowning.

I learned some very important lessons that day. Life can change in a second. Never take anything for granted. Never leave Cricket alone. And most important, spirits never die.

Bella & Cricket

Homewoods Rescue for the Wayward Hound
homewoodsrescue.com

Comfort

Soothing the Soul

A few years ago, I was visiting my great friend, food writer Elisabeth Luard, at her isolated fourteenth-century farmhouse in Wales. The rolling foothills of the Cambrian Mountains were emerald green and lush. Sheep were scattered as far as the eye could see, all covered in a wet mist. It was summertime, but you wouldn't know it unless, of course, you were Welsh. The weather was gloomy, with an ever-present, permeating, bone-chilling mist. Or, as we'd say in Maine, it was friggin' miserable.

After an afternoon of picking mushrooms in the forest, we retreated to Elisabeth's kitchen, where she started cooking and I whined about being damp. Elisabeth, being as British as they come, made me a hot cup of tea and topped it off with a generous helping of Glenfiddich 30 (year old) Whisky. "Drink up," she said. I did as I was told, noting that I preferred a shot of whiskey by itself to the milky version that was offered. To please me, a fire was lit in the sitting room, but the heat, like a ghostly presence, stayed strictly in that room, refusing to warm the rest of the house. I searched for comfort in a pet, only to find one cat, a mouser, who had no interest in me unless I was pouring her a saucer of cream. Eventually, I retreated to an upstairs bedroom that Elisabeth was kind enough to tell me was haunted. She tucked me into bed with my only consolation, a hot water bottle.

As I closed my eyes that night, ears alert for the sound of dragging chains, I thought about how much better that simple hot water bottle made me feel. My thoughts turned to my childhood. As wonderful as that hot, wobbly bottle of water felt, it didn't come close to the warmth my Golden Retriever, Sally, generated during the most frightening years of my life.

When I was seven years old, my Boxer, Bookie, died, and Sally joined our family. She was beautiful and lovely and kind. I'd rush home from school to be with her, preferring a long walk on the shore or an exploration together in the woods to riding bikes with friends. At home, I shared her with my sister and two brothers. She completed our happy family and made everything fun. Sally was also our champion, choosing to ride the mattress down the stairs with us instead of behind us, happily eating our unwanted liver as we slipped it to her under the dining table, and endlessly letting me entertain her as I sang along to David Cassidy, Carole King, and Three Dog Night. In the evening, Sally slept on the bed with me.

When I was ten years old, my perfect bubble popped. I came home from school one day, and there wasn't any dinner on the stove or warm cookies on the kitchen counter. There was only a note from my mother. She had left us.

As our family began a series of life-altering transitions, my one constant was Sally. I slept with my head on her stomach, my tears absorbed by her skin, finding a way to her heart.

Within twelve months, both of my parents had remarried. My brother Jim and I chose to stay with Dad and his new wife. Sally remained with us. We all adjusted and settled in, until one day, my mother's husband showed up, demanding that we go with him. He was drunk. He was angry. And he had a gun. My mother, apparently, was invoking her right to custody. My father intervened, and a lawyer was called. It was my mother's right. We had to go. I screamed for Sally, and she jumped into the car. As we drove away,

I looked back at my dad. He was crying. My world had, once again, collapsed. And it was going to get worse.

Later that day, Sally and I were ripped apart. I watched, helplessly screaming out, as she was taunted, kicked, and banished to a cold dog kennel. Jimmy and I joined my sister Katy and brother Billy in a room in the unheated section of the house.

The large, nicely appointed waterfront estate where my mother and her husband lived was surrounded by colorful gardens. But the veneer was eerily deceptive. There was a monster living inside.

One night, I woke to my stepfather hovering over me, his drool dripping on my face. My eyes opened, yet I remained frozen and silent. He had a revolver and a bullet. As he teetered in his drunken stupor, he placed the bullet in the chamber. "Let's see if tonight is your lucky night," he said. He spun the revolver, placed the gun to my head, and pulled the trigger. When it didn't go off, he mumbled to himself and stumbled out of the room—the same room I shared with my brothers and sister. I was grateful he'd chosen me instead of one of them.

While my mother was emotionally absent, Sally was not. When I dared, I found solace on the floor of the cold kennel with Sally, where all was safe and warm. It was as if she knew she was on a necessary journey and remained confidently introspective, never faltering with her love or her ability to lift my spirits. She knew the evil that surrounded us, yet she had a way of making it disappear. The moment I opened the kennel gate, we escaped into another world, even if it was only for a short time.

Sally's strength became mine, and a new persona emerged from the fearful teenager. I stopped crying and became angry. My defiance was noted, and I was shipped away to boarding school, ripped from my family once again and, more disturbingly, put in a position where I couldn't protect them.

For two years, I was forced to suffer silently. I missed my family, and my heart ached for Sally. And although we were apart, she remained my beacon of light and hope. She had taught me to prevail, and I'd made a promise to her. I would come back.

It was Thanksgiving, and I was with my family. Sally was still in the cold kennel, and I was at the dinner table. It was a simple thing. My gorgeous redheaded brother Bill asked permission to leave the table to get a glass of water. When he stood up and walked toward the kitchen, my stepfather picked up a knife and chucked it at his head. As it flew past Billy's ear, he froze. I stood up, walked upstairs to the bedroom, and started packing. My mother followed, asking what I was doing. I told her that I was leaving because she was killing everyone I loved and I hated her for it. She shut the bedroom door, grabbed my shoulders with her hands, and said, "Stay, for one more night. We'll all leave with you tomorrow." I couldn't believe it. My old mom was back! I don't know why she had stayed for so many years. Perhaps it was his good looks, wealth, or desire for her. All I knew was that the spell was broken. And the next day, after my stepfather left for work, my mother and I, my two brothers, my sister, his daughter, and two dogs packed into one car, and we ran away.

We escaped to my grandfather's cabin in northern Maine. We didn't have electricity or running water, but we were free of fear. Sally and I slept together again, swam in remote mountain streams, and took long walks in the woods.

Sally was everything to me—everything. She comforted me as I suffered, nurtured me as I grew, instilled in me the difference between right and wrong, and was my mother when my own was lost. Sally was my good in the world.

There's a well-known saying about children who are in abusive situations: Kids don't tell. It's true. I only told one adult what was happening to me when it was happening, a police officer. And nothing happened. But I told my dog everything. And she listened and responded. It was through Sally that I discovered the remarkable ability and willingness of a dog to comfort a person even in the midst of its own hardships.

Like many people, I've always been able to count on a dog. I've never truly felt the same way about people. I know I'm not alone, and I don't look at this as a bad thing. I think it's okay. We all have trials in life. It's what we learn from them that matters. I've learned never to underestimate the ability of a dog to provide comfort where a person can't.

Sally

"I have always wanted to be the man my dog thinks I am"

Gary Corneer

Two months after losing my thirteen-year-old chocolate Labrador to cancer, I began the search for another Lab. I was searching rescue sites on the Internet when I came across a picture that stopped me in my tracks. It was a chocolate Lab with piercing golden eyes and a big, blocky, beautiful head. The dog was at the Rimrock Humane Society in Roundup, Montana, one hundred sixty miles from my home. I called the Society and learned he was three years old and had been surrendered by his owners. They had kept him alone in a kennel for years after he failed to perform well in field trials and showed an aversion to hunting. His name was Gunner.

I had to meet this dog. I arranged to meet with the director at a "neutral" site in Roundup, a baseball diamond. After driving three hours, I pulled into the parking lot of the ballpark, grabbed a treat, opened the door to my pickup, and looked across the field. On the other side was the most beautiful Lab I'd ever seen. He took one look at me, sprinted across the field, took the treat, and immediately jumped into my truck. I guess you could say we found each other. We never looked back. On the long trip home Gunner became Gunny, and a fast-food ritual began. After stopping at McDonald's, I decided to share my fries with my new best friend, who was sitting in the backseat of the cab. As I handed each french fry backward, he gently took them from me. When we arrived home, I noticed he hadn't eaten them. Instead, he had chosen to place them neatly in a pile. I would soon find out that he didn't eat french fries unless they had catsup on them.

At the time of Gunny's adoption, I was teaching woodworking and construction at Bozeman High School in Bozeman, Montana. The next morning, I brought Gunny to school. He walked up to each student, leaning into them as if to say, "It's good to finally be here with you." It was as if he knew them and had never been away. When the kids went to work, he was mellow and just lay down beside me. He was the hit of the day.

The next day, I left him at home, thinking a nice fenced-in yard, toys, and my two Basset Hounds would be enough to keep him occupied until I got out of school. Wrong. Gunny was bored. He removed everything he could carry from the garage and dragged it into the backyard, including his blanket, bowl, toys, boots, and shoes.

Being the good "parent" I am, I decided to reward the bad behavior Gunny started coming to school with me every day. Most mornings, we drove through McDonald's, where I had to convince the servers that sausage patties weren't good for dogs. They quickly reverted to dog treats. At school, he became one of the class. His routine in the woodshop included wandering around during class time, stopping intermittently for a pat or a scratch under the chin. He had a blanket under my desk where he retreated. He was loved. A couple of the kids even built him a special bed for the club cab of my pickup truck.

Six years later, I applied for the job of dean of students and was offered the position. I assumed the school was hiring both of us. But the day of my first administrative meeting with our principal, assistant principals, assistant superintendent, and superintendent of schools, I left Gunny at home. When the assistant superintendent asked if Gunny needed his own e-mail to make sure he attended the next meeting, I knew we were in.

I am now the dean of students to the sophomore and senior high school kids, in a school with seventeen hundred students. My job is to get kids through high school without dropping out. It includes being a liaison among parents, teachers, and students and disciplining students when needed.

Handing out punishment isn't a pleasant part of the job. It's difficult, because kids' baggage often has to do with their home life and is beyond the school's ability to control. It's hard to discipline someone when you know the reasons they're acting the way they are and you can't do anything about it. Gunny is always there for them. He's a natural defuser. He absolutely loves everybody. Considering his own background, the dog never should have trusted again, but he does.

I had always been aware of Gunny's ability to comfort others, but one day, his gift was enlightening. There was a young lady in my office experiencing what I would guess was her worst day in high school. A police officer was also in the room with us. The girl had been caught punching another girl. She was failing classes and had troubles at home. She was pleading with us. "You don't understand. I have a hard life." As she argued, she had a total meltdown, crying so hard she had trouble catching her breath. As she struggled to breathe, Gunny quietly got up, walked over to her, put his head in her lap, and looked up at her. The moment was magic—absolutely magic.

She reached down and began stroking his head. Her crying stopped, and within minutes she was smiling.

I will never forget how Gunny changed the way that meeting was going. It was a simple act of kindness that changed everything. I have learned from Gunny that kindness and caring are not traits that are exclusively human. Dogs have the same qualities.

After disciplining my kids, I tell them that they've made a mistake, but everyone does. I let them know that when they come back to school after serving their detention or suspension, Gunny and I will not judge them; we're good. Gunny helps me live that promise.

There is an old quote that says, "I have always wanted to be the man my dog thinks I am." That's my goal. Gunny is helping me achieve it. He's a true friend and teacher to everyone. I'm just the lucky one who gets to take him home each night.

Gunny

Rimrock Humane Society
rimrockhumanesociety.org

Joshua and AJ

Bangor Humane Society
bangorhumane.org

"After the horror calmed down, we were asked to accept a gift"

Debbie Lander

O n January 21, 1991, a litter of beautiful Springer Spaniels arrived on earth. My sixteen-year-old son, Joshua, had seen the pups at his friend's house, and of course, he wanted one. He told me he had picked out a female, but we already had three dogs, so I said no.

A week later, on Super Bowl Sunday, my son was killed in an auto accident not far from home.

After the horror calmed down, my husband and I were asked to accept a gift. We were given the puppy my son had picked out. She was named Aja Jo (AJ). The first time I held her, I could feel Josh's love. I believed at that moment that this dog was an angel sent by our son to help us through what would be many long years of grief.

And she was. Over time, she taught us it was okay to be happy and to laugh. She kept us alive and helped us get through very rough times.

When AJ was ten, she began acting as if she didn't feel well. I took her to the vet, where she had every test imaginable, but they didn't find anything. Two years later, in the middle of the night, everything changed.

AJ woke me up and wanted to go out. But when she went out, she lay down on the grass and looked up at the sky. I went to her and lay with her, looking up at the stars. I don't know how or why, but I knew someone else was calling her, and she wanted to go. She was so unhappy. Something inside me knew it was time to let her go.

The next morning, on the long ride to the vet, we stopped at our usual place along a river where we always took time to play. I decided right then and there that I couldn't say good-bye. So we got back into the car, and I turned around, headed for home. And that's when she started crying and howling. She yelled at me, pleading for me to let her go. It was as if she was saying, "He's calling me."

I turned the car back around, and the moment I did, the howling stopped, and her tail started wagging. She was actually excited! I was amazed by this and wondered if I was imagining it all.

As I gazed into her eyes, I realized the least I could do for her was to do what she asked. She had carried us for twelve years. She knew we would be okay. I knew in my heart she was God's gift, my four-legged angel.

Once I let go of AJ, a sense of peace filled me, and I realized God and our son had sent her to us even before he left. I miss them both, but I know they're together.

"She hugged me"

Beth Lockhart

It was the third week of May in 2007, and my two children, Adam and Kurt, were moving out of the house. I had known Adam was leaving and had time to prepare, but when Kurt announced he was going, too, I realized I'd have an empty nest. It's a day you think you're ready for, but when it happens, it's emotional.

I was terribly distraught when they left. My husband was working nights that weekend and was sleeping. I didn't want to bother or wake him. So I went outside, sat down on the back steps, and started crying.

I'd left our five-month-old Golden Retriever, Sadie, behind in the house. But as I cried, I heard her crying and scratching at the door to get to me. I didn't want her to wake my husband, so I let her out. And that's when it happened.

As I sat there crying, Sadie jumped on my back. At first, I thought she wanted to play. I was in no mood. I just wanted to cry. And then, as I cried, with Sadie's warm body against my back, I felt a gentle squeeze, and I realized she was hugging me. She put her paws on my shoulders and pushed down from the top. She then nuzzled my neck with her nose. She wasn't wiggling around or playing with my hair. Her action was deliberate. I reached for my shoulder and touched one of her paws, and I felt it again: a squeeze, an actual hug.

The moment I realized what she was doing, I cried even harder. She was giving me the support I needed.

Sadie continued to hug me for several minutes until I stopped crying. It seemed like a long time for a puppy to remain still. It took me a few seconds to figure out what was happening, and when I realized it, I sat motionless. I hugged the paw that was on my right shoulder, not wanting the hug to stop. It's hard to explain how it felt, but it made me feel warm all over. Her hug was supportive and understanding, and it was a pure display of unconditional love. I was surprised at first, but when I felt the warmth of love she was giving me, a sense of peace washed over me. It was heavenly. I pulled her around and put her in my lap. She didn't wiggle or try to get away. She just lay there as I hugged her. And that's when the flood of tears came.

The memory of that one moment has given me the peace and strength to handle other trying times in my life. I look at her, and she lights up with life. She's my strength. This dog, who clearly understands the emotions of people, fills me with love.

Sadie

The Ark Animal Shelter
thearkpets.org

Olive

Greater Androscoggin Humane Society
gahumane.org

"A hell I never saw coming"

Jeff Gosselin

My wife discovered Olive on the Internet. She and her six lit-
termates had been left on a road in Tennessee in a box that
was duct-taped shut. Their mother was found sitting diligently beside the box. We adopted her sight unseen. When Olive arrived off
the eighteen-wheeler transport truck, we discovered she was a tan
and white spotted Catahoula Leopard Dog mix.

My twelve-year-old yellow Labrador, Algebra, didn't quite
know what to make of the twelve-week-old puppy. He had suffered
a stroke a month before, and everything had changed. I knew he
was on borrowed time. The first morning Olive was with us, I decided to take the dogs for a swim at a nearby pond. Algebra loved
the water and spent fifteen minutes wading in it. Olive didn't take
to it. She stood near the water's edge, looking quizzically at it. Two
hours later, Algebra had another stroke and died.

Days became weeks, and Olive clearly became my wife's dog.
She sat at her feet and loyally followed when she went to bed at
night. Even though I was the one to take Olive for long walks
every day, she remained true to my wife.

Seven months passed from the day Algebra left and Olive arrived, and I retired from teaching math for forty years. A month later, my life turned into a hell I never saw coming. My wife, the love of my life, left me and Olive, unannounced.

I was blindsided. She had always said we'd be married forever, and I believed it. Along with my own pain, it was very difficult to watch Olive sit hour after hour, looking out the window, waiting for her car to return.

It would have been easy to take the quitter's way out and take Olive to a shelter, but I'm not a quitter, and it was never considered. Olive had been abandoned twice now, and that was not going to happen again on my watch, regardless of the pain I was going through.

I didn't know how to make myself happy, but I knew how to make Olive happy. I started taking her for extra-long walks in the woods on snowmobile, cross-country skiing, and running trails. It gave me a sense of purpose. Letting her run in the woods turned out to be therapeutic for both of us.

At night, instead of going to my bedroom, I camped out in front of the stone fireplace, lying on dog beds and watching the Celtics with Olive curled up by my side. It was quite comfortable, both physically and mentally. For three weeks, this was our routine until we moved back upstairs.

Olive saved my life. She was the only reason I was able to stay away from a very dark place after my wife left. Today we continue to make the first event of every day her unbounded walk in the woods. My most important goal has been to provide her with the best quality of life I can, to make sure she's never abandoned again. I have a feeling that her goal is the same for me.

I've learned something very important from Olive. Love doesn't have to come from another person to be meaningful.

"The gentleman was near death"

Penny Black

When I first saw Zak, he was four and a half and had been off the Seabrook dog track for eight months. He'd been rescued by a couple devoted to Greyhounds and was patiently waiting for a home. I was looking for a gentle dog, a companion for my blind Cocker Spaniel, Ebby. The rescue had four males. I looked at all of them but couldn't make a decision.

The next day, I called Carol, the woman who ran the rescue, and asked her who she thought would be a good fit for Ebby. She told me that Zak was always passed over for adoption because of his unusually large size. She said he had a wonderful nature and was the mellowest Greyhound that had ever come through the rescue. Although his size was a deterrent, I didn't need to hear any more. He was the dog for us.

Zak's gentle ways quickly became apparent. He was calm, kind, and engaging. Ebby often bumped into him as she made her way around the house, and he was patient with her. He didn't make a fuss, clearly understanding her predicament. They even swapped dog bones without incident. He was perfect for her.

He was also perfect for my mother. Mom was a no-nonsense, practical person who had a way with dogs. She liked Zak right away and figured he just plain understood everything we felt and said. Mom had always maintained that life was too short to do "whatever." So, just before she died, she set me on a mission when she said, "You need to share this dog. He does wonders for people."

I thought about what Mom said and decided she was right. Even though time had passed and Zak was now nine years old, I needed to share him.

Zak and I began working as a pet therapy team at the nearby Veterans Administration hospital. Zak's large size and gentle manner made him a big hit with the veterans we visited. He was especially good with hospice patients, standing quietly next to them while they patted his head and often talked about their own pets.

One day, we arrived to find out that one of Zak's favorite patients had passed, and a different family was occupying his room. Inside, a husband lay listless on the bed while his wife sat quietly next to him. We hesitated outside the door. But the wife noticed Zak and sent a nurse into the hallway to invite us in.

It was clear the gentleman in the bed was near death. He was very still, curled up on his side with one hand on top of the covers. His wife stepped up to him and quietly told him he had a visitor. I could tell she was hoping for a response, but there wasn't any.

Zak stepped up to the bed. Because of his height, his head was level with the man's body. Then he did something he'd never done before. He extended his long neck like a giraffe and leaned forward until his head reached the man's exposed hand. Then, without prompting, he gave the hand a gentle lick. The hand moved slightly, and the man made a low guttural sound. It was enough to bring his wife to her feet, speaking her husband's name. She was smiling when she turned and thanked me for coming, and then she looked down at Zak and thanked him personally.

You might not think there's anything special about a dog licking, but Zak wasn't a licker. He didn't even give kisses to me! Remarkably, he elicited a response from a dying man. And while that moment was visibly small to me, it meant the world to someone else.

As we walked out, I was proud of Zak and deeply moved by his compassion. It was a "wow" moment. I looked at Zak and said, "If you don't take another right step in your life, what you just did was incredible."

Three months later, I lost my Zak to a brain tumor, something he most likely had for a long time but kept to himself. Maybe he was too big to be a good racer and too big for adopters to see his potential, but I think that maybe he was just plain saved for me—a gift from God, a gentle giant in a Greyhound suit.

Through Zak, I was able to help veterans but also help myself by being useful to others. He showed me how big an impact we can have on the lives of others with just a simple lick of the hand, and that special gifts come in all suits and sizes. My mother was right. Zak did do wonders for people.

Therapy Dogs
therapydogs.com

Coco

Atlanta Pet Rescue and Adoption
atlantapetrescue.org

"The dogs that lived outside the orphanage"

Dee Thompson

In 2004, I adopted a thirteen-year-old girl from an orphanage in Khabarovsk, Russia. Alesia had been removed from the care of her alcoholic birth mother at the age of six because of severe neglect and abuse. Her birth mother never contacted her again. Her father had left when she was a baby.

Not long after my daughter, Alesia, came home, my mother and I purchased a house together, and Alesia was given her own room. As exciting as this was for her, she was afraid to sleep by herself. At that time, she was still unsure she could trust me, her granny, or any other adult. Grown-ups had always let her down.

On the first night in her bedroom, Alesia took my mother's tiny Yorkie-Poo, Coco, to bed with her, and a ritual began. They crawled into bed together every night, and once Alesia was asleep, Coco would quietly jump off the bed, go downstairs, and get into bed with my mother, whom she had slept with since she was a puppy.

Alesia treated Coco like a doll at first, putting different outfits on her and singing songs to her in Russian. Coco seemed to sense that Alesia needed her and was always willing to be cuddled and played with for hours. There was trust and love there.

A year passed, and Coco was diagnosed with Ehlers-Danlos syndrome, a rare disease that caused her skin to tear easily. The vet advised that most pet owners put their dogs down when they got the disease. We couldn't do that. But Coco could no longer go outside, for fear that if she brushed against a pine cone, it might break her skin. And she couldn't be groomed professionally.

The bond between Alesia and Coco strengthened. I watched as my Russian daughter, speaking little English, nurtured her sick friend by feeding, cuddling, and gently playing ball with her. Alesia took on the task of bathing Coco in the kitchen sink and then, sitting patiently on the floor, would carefully snip her hair one curl at a time. While Alesia supported Coco with unending compassion, Coco did the same for her. I think Coco was a canine angel to Alesia when she was lonely and scared.

It took me quite some time to realize the importance of Alesia's relationship with Coco. When she began to speak English, Alesia told me she never felt anyone loved her except the dogs that lived outside the orphanage. Food was scarce there, but she would save portions of her meals to give to the homeless dogs. She even made a "house" of cardboard for her favorite dog, Greta, so that Greta could give birth to her puppies under shelter. Those homeless dogs provided comfort and love to my daughter in a place where they were scarce.

Alesia felt no love from any human in Russia, and yet she always had empathy and love for the dogs who, like herself, were abandoned. They, in turn, loved her unconditionally. Without them, my daughter may never have experienced the joy of loving another being. I'm grateful she's always known love in the form of a dog.

"I wanted to give up on life"

Lynn Nobil

The call came in the middle of the night. The police were on their way. My seventeen-year-old son, Erik, had died in a car accident. He was one week away from starting school at the Berklee School of Music.

It was a family tragedy, and everyone suffered—my parents, my husband, my daughter, Kiersten, and our Boxer, Bo. Erik and Bo had a nightly ritual of playing and roughhousing together. That came to an abrupt end when Erik was killed.

The truth is, everything ended. I went into a tailspin. When I was alone during the day, I was beyond despair. There were no words to describe it. I had to get up in the morning but could barely function. I did all the things people in my situation do. I went to a therapist. After several sessions of baring my soul, she told me that everyone would die. That wasn't the answer for me. I tried Valium and sleep medication. They made me feel worse. I tried to move forward by returning to school, where I was working on a degree in psychology. But once I got on campus, every student looked like my son. I couldn't do it. Quite honestly, I wanted to give up on life.

And while I certainly wasn't there for anyone else, especially my daughter, our dog, Bo, was there for me. He interpreted my every emotion and need. Bo pushed me to get outside and focus on walking instead of crying. When I would cry, he would go out of his mind trying to figure out what to do to stop it. He'd pace back and forth anxiously. And sometimes, when I'd collapse on the ground from pain, he'd snuggle up and lick and nudge me in the face, trying to cheer me up the best way he could.

But his comfort didn't stop the suffering, and time wasn't a healer. One day, after thinking of the many ways I could end my life by making it look like an accident, I came up with a plan. While walking Bo, I'd put him on the sidewalk while I walked in the road, hoping to be hit by a car. My family would think my death was an accident and not a suicide.

With this plan in place, I began walking in the road with Bo on the sidewalk. But every time I did this, Bo would use all his strength to pull me out of the road. Time after time, I would step into the road, only to be yanked back, again and again. My plan was foiled, and I was forced to move forward.

I have a beautiful daughter who still needs her mom. My family and friends, who have been a great support system, need me, too. I'm grateful now for every day that I'm alive. I'll never forget that Bo was there in my darkest hours, guiding me from the depths of personal despair to a higher place. He was there to prevent me from giving up and taking my life.

Bo and Erik are together now. I find comfort in knowing that.

I learned from Bo how closely we're connected to animals. There's a silent language between us. Bo made me realize that animals can offer comfort in ways that humans can't.

Society for the Prevention of Cruelty to Animals of Hancock County
spcahancockcounty.org

Baldwin

Lange Foundation
langefoundation.com

"Who's this little doctor?"

Susan Hartzler

I'm a dog lover—have always been one, will always be one. But never in my wildest dreams would I have believed how a dog could not only touch my life but also touch the lives of many others.

I wasn't in the market for a dog. I was volunteering at the Lange Foundation, a no-kill shelter in Los Angeles, when I met a mop of jet black curls the size of a shoebox. His name was Baldwin, and he was a Hungarian Sheep Dog known as a Puli. He made it clear that he wanted me, but I wasn't sure. When I came back the next day, he wagged not only his little stump of a tail but also his entire body. He knew from the moment he saw me that I was his. Now I knew it, too.

I picked him up and inhaled his earthy puppy scent that reminded me of sunshine and happiness. His fate was decided at that very moment. He would bring that sunshine and happiness where it was needed most, to sick children in hospitals.

But before that happened, he needed training. He trained in sheep herding and agility, winning awards for his speed and accuracy. After that, he went to school and received his certification to be a therapy dog.

My friend Marilyn founded the dog therapy program at the County General Hospital in downtown Los Angeles. I was thrilled when she chose Baldwin and me to be part of her program.

I'll never forget our first visit. I dressed Baldwin in green scrubs, complete with a purple stethoscope. He didn't mind being dressed up. He appeared to sense that he was embarking on an important mission, and the outfit was just part of the deal. I was a bit nervous. This was a new environment, with very different smells and sounds. Baldwin was a high-energy Sheep Dog. He knew lots of tricks to entertain children. He could roll over, high-five, and sneeze on command. But there was a chance he might get too excited. I brought a bag of treats to keep him distracted in case he got into trouble.

When we got out of the car at the hospital, Baldwin immediately pulled me toward the entrance. I didn't even know how to get inside. How did he? That was my first sign that he knew where we were going and what our mission was. We got into the elevator, and a nurse wearing matching scrubs took one look at him and broke into hysterics. When the elevator doors opened on the sixth floor, Leita, the head of the program, was waiting for us. "Who's this little doctor?" she asked. "We'll have to get him an official badge." She reached down to pet Baldwin, but he gave her his paw to shake instead. "Oh, a formal hello, I see," she said as she shook his paw.

"Dr. Baldwin will be visiting with a special little girl who's waiting in the playroom. She just got out of chemotherapy, so we can't have her around any of the other kids because of germs."

We were led to the children's playroom. Inside was a tiny seven-year-old girl sitting on a couch in a wrinkled hospital gown.

Her eyes were sunken in and surrounded by thick black circles. She looked gaunt and tired. Her pale complexion gave her a look of transparency. Her name was Maria.

Maria's mother sat next to her, holding her bony hand, caressing it slowly, singing softly to her child as she rocked back and forth. Maria didn't move. She sat quietly, with a blank stare on her face as if she were in a trance. They both looked lost in the room made for twenty kids, with computer games beeping, a large-screen TV blaring, and brightly colored murals on the walls.

As we entered, all of the distractions disappeared. I focused my attention on Maria and her mother, taking note of the IV in the girl's arm. Leita spoke softly to the mother in Spanish, and they both gently touched the young girl, bringing her awareness back to the room.

When Maria looked up and saw Baldwin, her face began to transform. She smiled slightly and relaxed, taking a deep breath that brought some color into her face.

I asked the little girl, in broken Spanish, if she wanted Baldwin to sit next to her. She nodded her head up and down. Baldwin immediately hopped up on the couch and laid his entire body across hers. I was mortified! What if he hurt her? I didn't expect him to do this, but it was too late, he just did it.

But as much as I was mortified, Maria seemed to like it. I made sure her IV was clear of him and then sat across from them and watched. Maria rubbed Baldwin's chin until he put his head down, sighed, and closed his eyes. In no time, with Baldwin sprawled across her, she was breathing deeply, with more color coming into her face with each inhalation.

For the next hour, I watched as Maria gently stroked Baldwin's fur, her little hand moving in the same direction over and over again. It made me think of someone's fingers praying with rosary beads, and in my mind, I started repeating, "Hail Mary, full of grace, the Lord is with thee." And as I realized that I was repeating the same mantra over and over again, I realized what I was witnessing: grace in motion.

Baldwin didn't move an inch the whole time we were in that room. Here was this high-energy dog who ran agility courses and herded sheep, a dog who made me throw balls and Frisbees for him for hours. Rarely did he snuggle with me. But here in the oncology ward, he was doing exactly what had to be done, exactly what a sick little girl needed at that very moment.

From this experience, I understood that Baldwin was tuned into something far greater than I could ever comprehend. I was just his facilitator at the end of a leash.

Here's what I know that I didn't before: it's okay to love dogs as much as I do. I have come out of the closet as the dog lover I truly am, and I have no shame!

Intuition

The Theory of Truth

World-renowned scientist Rupert Sheldrake has confirmed through his experiments with dogs that telepathy is real and that man and dog can communicate from great distances apart. If you're a dog lover, you already know this. You also know that dogs have the ability to sense things you can't.

As easily as my generation has embraced the computer and the Internet, with time and acceptance, we'll see and understand what some scientists already know: there are bonds between species that encompass the past and transcend space and time. Sheldrake calls it morphic resonance. We use the terms *sixth sense* or *intuition* to describe it. Whatever it might be, it's a form of telepathy that's not yet widely recognized by human beings but is clearly inherent in dogs.

In my early twenties, I was working as a morning news anchor and reporter at a CBS television affiliate in Bangor, Maine. I had four dogs and lived in a tiny two-room apartment. I was struggling, making less than ten thousand dollars a year. The dogs ate rice and dry dog food, and my diet wasn't much different.

To make matters worse, my apartment building was transitional housing for the mentally ill after their release from the local psychiatric hospital. There were often terrifying sounds coming from the other three apartments. I felt terrible about leaving the dogs all day in that frightening place, but it was the only rental that allowed pets. It certainly wasn't the glamorous life I'd expected to live as a television news reporter. To keep them company, I always left the TV on for them, tuned into my station.

One day, a girlfriend came for a visit from out of town. While I worked, she stayed with the dogs at the apartment. When I returned on the first day, she told me the most amazing story. She said that at 7:20, five minutes before I went on the air to deliver the morning news, my all-white American Spitz, Mary, hopped up on my very tall poster bed and sat in front of the television set. She then proceeded to watch me on the news. When the news finished, she hopped off the bed. She did the same thing again just before I went on the air at 8:20.

This was my first glimpse into Mary's extrasensory perception. I'd known she liked to watch *Lassie* on television, but I'd written her interest off as a keen ability to understand Lassie's barks.

But six years later, I couldn't discount Mary's intuitive abilities. I was living with a kind man named Jim who happened to be a funeral director. We lived in a very large Colonial, on the second story, just up a floor from the funeral home and up two floors from the casket showroom and embalming rooms. It was a very spacious, beautiful apartment. Its only drawback was that it was spooky.

I was now down to two dogs, Mary and Philophal. Philophal was a Terrier cross I rescued off the streets in Ogden, Utah. Mary had been a stray, found eating garbage near an Air Force base in Clearfield, Utah.

I had left the dogs alone in the apartment plenty of times. They were both more than ten years old and were pretty relaxed. One day, while I was shopping, I received an urgent call from one of the funeral directors. A funeral was in session, and the dogs were barking incessantly. No one could calm them. I rushed home and met Jim at the back stairs. We ran up together and witnessed the same thing when we opened the door.

Mary and Philophal were in the hallway that led to the funeral parlor. They were standing opposite each other, as if a person stood between them, and they were both looking upward and barking ferociously. Our entry didn't discourage them. They were clearly protecting their territory from an intruder. We called their names. Their eyeballs flickered toward us in acknowledgment, and then they immediately turned back to something that was very real to them but invisible to us. And then it was as if the entity started walking toward the door. Both dogs turned in the same direction, barking and following the same thing until they were led to the door to where the funeral was in progress. They both sniffed frantically at the door and then at the thin gap between the door and the floor. A moment later, they turned around and greeted us.

If there was ever a time I was speechless, this was it. Jim and I looked at each other, and it was rarely mentioned again. There are some things we as humans don't really want to tap into, especially when living in a funeral home.

Philophal, Mary, and Pete, as reindeer

"I saw something that took my breath away"

Susan Lilly

My dog Boomer, a Nova Scotia Duck Tolling Retriever mix, is a pleaser. He always wants to do his family right. His big sister Riley is a mix of breeds and looks like a small German Shepherd. Both are rescue dogs and are a big part of our family. We live in Telluride, Colorado, and hike together nearly every day.

In June 2004, we were walking on our river trail, as we often do. The river was flowing incredibly hard, as the snow from the mountains was melting. As usual, Riley stepped over the side of the riverbank to take a drink of water. But this time, she slipped off a rock and into the mad-flowing rapids. Immediately, her body went vertical, disabling her from being able to swim her way to safety. She spun around and around, paws aimlessly splashing in the rapids, with a look of helpless horror in her eyes.

After a quick, terrifying assessment, I ran as fast as I could in my flip-flops down the river trail, with the intention of jumping into the shallow river to intercept her from a certain drowning. I ran, looking back frequently to be sure to go far enough to catch

72

her. The third time I looked back, I saw something that took my breath away. Boomer, our ten-month-old puppy, had made his way to a rock on the river's edge and had Riley's neck in his mouth.

After securing his grip, he tugged her with a sort of gentle but ferocious sense of urgency out of the river, through the bushes, and onto the river trail. And then, without releasing her, he shook her back and forth, almost as a reprimand. She was safe, and Boomer was our hero for life.

From this experience, I realized there is almost a sixth sense that dogs and perhaps other animals have that clues them into danger and other intangible stimuli. I'm comforted in knowing the extraordinary things dogs, and in this case Boomer, can do in a largely human world.

Boomer & Riley

Second Chance Humane Society
secondchancehumanesociety.org

"I saved her
and she saved me"

Joy Peterkin

The first week of October 2004, my husband, Salem, and I were coming out of the doctor's office at the local mall when a young woman, holding a basket, approached us. She asked if we'd be interested in buying a puppy. We hesitated. We had lost our dearly loved Shih Tzu a year and a half before and had decided not to get another dog.

We are both animal lovers and couldn't resist looking at the puppies in the basket. The woman explained that she was in dire straits. She said her husband had been hurt in an accident, and they didn't have any money. The only thing she had were the puppies.

When we looked into the basket, there were three tiny puppies crawling around. One was much smaller than the other two, and I picked her up. She fit in the palm of my hand. When I put her up to my neck, she snuggled right in. She had my heart at that moment. We purchased her for twenty-five dollars.

The next day, I took her to the veterinarian, who confirmed

that she was most likely a Chihuahua and that she was about four weeks old.

We didn't know what to name her. One day, I looked into the box she was kept in and said, "Well, aren't you a little bit of a thing?"

"You just named her," Salem said.

So, Little Bit she became. At the time, she weighed a tiny eight ounces. We came to love her very much.

Eleven months after Little Bit came into our lives, we lost our home and all of our possessions in Hurricane Katrina. Little Bit helped us keep our sanity.

Four months later, we moved out of our Federal Emergency Management Agency trailer and relocated to another state. We were just settling into our new life when Little Bit started behaving strangely. She would get up in my lap and nose my right breast. Before this, she had always snuggled up inside my robe in the morning while I drank coffee and read the paper. Now she didn't cuddle, she just nosed my breast. I started to notice that it hurt when she bumped me. I felt around but didn't find anything.

After two weeks of Little Bit nosing my breast, I decided to see the doctor. I asked for a mammogram and told him about my dog's behavior. I was scheduled for the mammogram, and sure enough, they found a spot on my right breast that didn't look right. A biopsy proved it was cancer. It turned out to be so small that even the surgeon couldn't feel it. I was told it was the size of a small pea and was located under my nipple.

I was operated on three weeks later. The lumpectomy went well, and there were no surprises.

If God had not been watching over me and sent me that little puppy, I would probably have been in much worse shape by the time the lump was found. As it was, I only had to endure seven weeks of radiation. I have now been cancer-free for three and a half years.

Little Bit has never nosed my breast since I had the cancer removed. I guess the truth is that I saved her and she saved me.

Greater Androscoggin Humane Society
gahumane.org

"I was woken by a jolt"

Gloria Wardrum

In 1956 and 1957, there was a string of brutal murders of young children in the metropolitan area of Chicago. I was nineteen at the time, living with my family and working as a bookkeeper. My best friend was a multicolored curly-haired Airedale Terrier named Ginger. She slept on my bed with me, curled up against the backs of my knees. We were very close.

Ginger loved everyone and always greeted each person with a wag of her tail or a kiss, sometimes both. She was a loving and friendly family dog who never met a stranger she didn't like—until one summer evening.

After coming home from work, I almost always took Ginger for a walk. One day, I came home particularly tired. I didn't really want to go for a walk, but it was a beautiful day, and Ginger deserved to go out. We ended up at a park near my home. No one else was there, not a soul. It was dinnertime, so it didn't seem strange to me that the park was empty. It was very peaceful. I sat down with my back against a tree and fell asleep with Ginger's leash wrapped around my wrist.

I was woken by a jolt. Ginger was frantically pulling away from me, her leash tugging my arm. She was growling in a way I'd never heard her growl before. The hair on her back was standing straight up. I looked toward where she was looking. In the distance, a man was approaching us. He was holding a rope or something similar, and he was twisting it between his hands. Ginger was going wild. He kept walking toward us, and she kept yanking at the leash, trying to get to him. As he got closer, she growled fiercely, showing her teeth. I was terrified. I stood up, not knowing what to do. The sun was going down, it was getting dark, and I was alone except for my dog, who had never reacted this way to anyone before.

The man stopped twenty feet from us and asked, "Does that dog bite?"

I responded quickly, "You're darned right she does."

The man then circled us, incensing Ginger even more. She

Ginger

Orphans of the Storm Animal Shelter
orphansofthestorm.org

never took her eyes off him and continued to growl. She didn't settle down until he sauntered away and was completely out of sight.

Once home, I told my family what had happened and then set the event aside, appreciative of the fact that Ginger had been with me.

Shortly afterward, fifteen-year-old Judith Mae Andersen was murdered and dismembered. Her body was found three miles away from the park where Ginger and I had encountered the stranger. Judith Mae was last seen walking home from a friend's house after dark.

I might not be here today if it weren't for Ginger. She knew something evil was walking toward us that day. I am forever grateful to God for sending her to protect me.

Hope

Massachusetts Society for the Prevention of Cruelty to Animals
mspca.org

"She always had a sixth sense"

Judie Noonan Tardiff

A few months after my husband, Bob, died, our black Labrador Retriever, Tyler, joined him. Hope, my affectionate, protective, always hungry Lab, and I were alone now.

Nine months after Bob's death, at the urging of friends, I started dating. Hope had always been friendly and pleased to meet new people, but she was not happy with any of my suitors.

My first date was a very handsome and charming gentleman who forgot he was still married. Hope growled at the sight of him. She knew!

The next man was a four-hundred-pound basketball coach I met on a blind date who thought it was appropriate to ask to have sex immediately upon walking through the door of my house. When Hope was introduced to him, she stood her ground and barked, providing a protective barrier between him and me. She proceeded to bark continuously, until he couldn't stand it anymore and left. I wasn't impressed with him, either.

When I brought Randy home, I warned him in advance that Hope might not be friendly. I told him that my dog was my bodyguard and might sound fierce but wouldn't hurt him. As was customary, Hope was at the door the moment she heard the lock turn. I opened the door and greeted her with my usual "Hey, Hopie," my hand moving gently back and forth over the top of her head. Randy said hi to her, and she quickly began sniffing him, with her tail wagging so fast her butt wiggled. Much to my shock, he held out his hand, and she started licking it like crazy. They became fast friends, and for the rest of the night, Hope sat next to Randy instead of me. It was love at first sight.

Randy and I were married two years later. Hope is his best bud. She's always had a sixth sense about the goodness of people. She's always been right. I think dogs are better judges of character than we are.

"The hair literally stood up on the back of both our necks"

Deborah Boies

O ur "Molly the Messenger," as my husband, Bob, and I often
called her, had a unique ability from the time she was a tiny,
pudgy, black and tan Doberman puppy. She seemed to know things
that our other dogs often ignored or just didn't see or hear. Molly
was consistently in touch with her surroundings. She never missed
a thing that was going on at our Morgan horse farm.

Try as we might, we could never make Molly a house dog. She
preferred the freedom of coming and going around the farm. She
was primal when it came to patrolling her area and those she felt
were her charges, which included everyone living on the farm.
Molly's instinctive powers were acute. She was always guiding us,
and I feel she was being guided, too.

I first noticed Molly's ability early one morning when she
greeted me with a few extra wags of her nub tail. She was particularly anxious for me to get to the barn quickly, prompting me
to follow her by staring at me, wagging her nub, starting toward

the barn, and then coming back to me. Once confident that I was in tow, she ran ahead, put her paws up on the bars of the second stall window, and peered inside. As she stood there, she looked back at me, motioning me with her smile and lifted brow to hurry. I walked up to find a new foal had just been born to a mare that hadn't been due for two more weeks. Molly the Messenger gave us the news.

Another time, in the evening, Molly was anxious. She wouldn't settle down. I was watching her from the house. She would run to the barn, then run back to the house and run back to the barn again. I decided to walk to the barn to see what she was monitoring. Molly led the way. She took me to the corner of a horse stall, where one of our barn cats was lying in a pile of pine shavings. She was in the throes of a seizure and was dying. Molly the Messenger had communicated to us that someone was in trouble.

While Molly's extraordinary perception was often aimed at letting us know something was going on with one of the animals on the farm, that wasn't always the case. One summer night, her attention turned to us. It was the middle of the night, and Bob and I were in bed when we heard a frantic scratching at the garage door to the house. I figured it was Molly. I got up to reprimand her— to tell her everything was fine and that she could relax and quit scratching. Bob followed. As I opened the door, the hair literally stood up on the backs of our necks, and simultaneously, there was an explosive crack that rattled the house and then a bright flash of light that swooshed through the garage. Molly bolted past me, and I followed. As we reached the hallway in the center of the house, I could smell a pungent burning odor. With Molly in the lead, Bob and I searched the house to see if it was on fire. It wasn't. What we did find was that lightning had struck the tree directly outside our bedroom. It obliterated the tree, sending shards like spears through the screens in our bedroom windows.

The next morning, it was clear what had happened judging by the black streak that ran from what used to be the tree to the corner of our house and to our bedroom. If Molly hadn't scratched persistently at the door, we would have been in our bedroom when the lightning struck.

Sadly, we lost Molly too soon. She was only seven when she crossed the bridge. Her memory has not faded. Her nub tail still wags in my mind, and the gift she gave us is priceless. Trust your instincts. They will not fail you. The guiding of those instincts comes from a spiritual place.

Molly

Pilots N Paws
pilotsnpaws.org

"Everyone in the room was shocked"

Kay Neslage

Arnie was a grace-filled, soulful, divine presence of a yellow Labrador Retriever whose favorite thing to do was go to work visiting terminally ill children. If he could have driven to the hospital, he'd have gone without me.

I was an administrator for an outpatient rehabilitation center when Arnie and I began our work together in pet therapy. At the time, pet therapy was considered a recreational therapy and was not always recognized for its medical, emotional, and physical benefits. Arnie went through a training program with Therapy Dogs International and started out at my facility in Lubbock, Texas. Arnie's job was to help people recovering from illness and accidents improve their physical capabilities. In a nutshell, Arnie played a lot of ball with the patients.

There were many "aha" moments during our time together, but I knew Arnie had a divine presence when we worked with a three-year-old boy named Trey who had cancerous brain tumors.

Trey lived in New Mexico. After his diagnosis, his father deserted him and his mother, Becky. They were sent to Covenant Children's Hospital in Lubbock for Trey's treatments. When Arnie and I met Trey and Becky, they were alone and away from home.

There was an instant bond between Arnie and Trey. Our initial visit consisted of an exchange on the floor of Trey's hospital room. Arnie lay down next to him, and Trey shared his toys and crayons with the dog. After witnessing the interaction between the two, Trey's oncologist, Dr. Melanie Oblender (Dr. O), deemed Arnie

Arnie and Kay

Highland Lakes Society for the Prevention of Cruelty to Animals
highlandlakesspca.org

a positive mechanism to calculate Trey's brain function by his responses to Arnie. She also noted that Arnie was a respite after a series of painful treatments and long days for both Trey and his mom. We were asked to become regular visitors. It was our pleasure.

Each day, when we walked through the door of Trey's room, we were greeted with smiles and treats of food, such as bacon and sausage that Trey saved from his hospital meals for Arnie. This little family of two had barely anything, and yet they were giving and full of love. I never heard a negative word from Trey. He was always pleasant, even with all of the pain of the tumors and the therapy. He never said anything about hurting, hunger, home, or his suffering. He talked about his love for his own dog at home, a Pit Bull named Disaster, and for the cartoon character Scooby-Doo. And every time we left, he always told Arnie how much he loved him.

One unforgettable day, Dr. O paged us to the pediatric intensive care unit (PICU) of the University Medical Center. I was told Trey was in a coma. Dr. O wanted Arnie there to help her monitor Trey's brain function when he came out of the coma. Arnie had never been to the PICU at this hospital, yet as we entered the unit, with its long hallway, he ignored all of the rooms and went directly to the room where Trey was hooked up to numerous machines.

Arnie walked right up to the tall bed, jumped onto it, and spread himself across Trey's chest, wires and all. Everyone in the room was shocked. It was way out of character for Arnie. He usually scanned the periphery of a room upon entering, sniffed around the bed, and then greeted his patient. Not this time. I moved him off, pushing him to the side of his friend, but he refused and put his big paws and head back on Trey's chest, insistent on holding him down. The doctor was there and instructed me to leave him there.

She had complete faith that Arnie knew what he was doing. At that moment, Trey had his first seizure.

As the medical personnel rushed into the room, Arnie hopped off the bed and sat down near the door. While the ICU nurses responded, Dr. O, Becky, and I cried. Our tears were immediate and flowing. We all knew what we'd witnessed. Arnie had sensed what all the monitors couldn't, and the moment help arrived, he stepped aside.

About six months later, Dr. O called to tell me that all efforts had been exhausted and that Trey would be going home to New Mexico for hospice care. We went for one last visit, to say goodbye. The ambulance opened its doors, and Trey was put in on a stretcher. Arnie didn't hesitate and jumped in after him. It was as if he knew it was the last time they'd be together. After Trey left, Arnie became depressed. I tried to cheer him up but to no avail. I felt sure he was sensing Trey's impending death.

A few weeks later, Trey succumbed to the cancer. Arnie sat near Becky during the funeral, providing the comforting love only an angel can dispense.

When your work involves the sick, the cross-section of suffering involves everyone. Arnie and I saw children of all races and economic backgrounds, and Arnie dove right into each room with the same grace. He did not judge anyone by age, race, or aptitude. His love and compassion were unconditional. Arnie was a lesson in perfect love for us all.

"I told you I'd give you a sign of my love when I died"

Joyce Cutten

My husband, Bill, died in September 1996. Prior to his unexpected death, we'd often discussed whether communication after death was possible. We had a great rapport with each other in life, which perhaps is only natural after sixty years of togetherness. But he was a complete skeptic about this "life after life" business.

On a couple of occasions, I suggested to him that when either of us died, we should try to communicate with the one left behind. He said I was a nut but agreed to it.

Before any of this happened, a family came to live across the road from us. They owned a little female Rough Haired Terrier named Skye. She was nine years old, and I can tell you, she was no canine beauty.

Occasionally, Skye would wander over to our garden with a ball in her mouth and look pleadingly at Bill, inviting him to throw the ball for her to chase. He would oblige, and they became great friends. I would often see her resting with her muzzle on his knee, looking lovingly at him. She wouldn't come inside the house, and we didn't give her meals, as we didn't want to entice her away from her family. Sometimes, as a treat, we would give her a bone to chew on, but that was all. I think she was lonely. She kindly acknowledged me with a wag of her tail, but it was Bill she adored and even flirted with. We'd always loved dogs, but this was the first time we were actually adopted by one.

Before long, Skye would leave her house in the morning and come to us for the day, playing with Bill as he worked in the garden. She would go back to her house to greet her family upon their return home from work and to receive her meal.

Without warning, Bill became ill one day and was taken by ambulance to the hospital. Skye immediately camped out on the doormat of the house and refused to leave. She would lift her sad eyes up to mine and then place her nose on her paws, steadily watching me. She knew that Bill had died. Her sad expression told me everything. I couldn't figure out how she had sensed what had happened.

Skye had ignored me until the day Bill died. From that day forward, she camped out on our doormat and would not leave. On the day of Bill's funeral, many of our family and friends came back to our house for tea and such. They all had to step over my guardian as they entered.

My definitive sign from Bill came the first morning after his passing, when Skye presented me with a gift, delivered to my feet with love in her eyes. It was a gum nut from the eucalyptus tree in the garden where she and Bill had played their daily game of ball. Every morning after that, Skye would bring me a gift the moment she knew I was up. The gift was always a gum nut or a gum leaf. I felt the gift was from Bill. He was a quiet man, and she knew him well. It was a miraculous thing. It was as if he was telling me, "I told you I'd give you a sign of my love when I died."

Skye was understanding and compassionate to me after Bill's passing. She didn't let a day go by without the loving gesture of a gift. She never expected me to throw it for her to chase; it was clearly a gift from Bill through Skye. And while I hadn't been the one she played with, she took up residence, day and night, on the front mat as my guardian. And that is where she stayed until she died. A few weeks after Bill passed, Skye's owner took her for a walk on a busy road without a leash, and Skye was hit and killed by a car.

I now believe that the love from a dog to a man can extend to man's other best friend, his wife. I have experienced it. I also know we are blessed in life by people and by pets. I certainly have been.

Dogs' Refuge Home
dogshome.org.au

"If there are no dogs in heaven, I don't want to go"

Glenwood McNabb

I am a retired high school teacher and principal and have lived alone for quite some time. For many years, my constant companion was a Keeshond named Cinder. She was an affectionate old girl who loved children and animals and taking rides in the car. We would visit friends several times a week, and occasionally, when it was time to go home, she'd refuse. She wanted to stay and play with my friends and their pets. On those days, I'd let her spend the night, to have a slumber party. The next morning, I'd retrieve her, and she was always ready to come home. It was one of the many things she did that amused me.

When Cinder was fifteen years old, knowing our friendship would come to an end sooner than later, a lady friend gave me a six-week-old Pomeranian puppy I named Zoey. I laid her beside Cinder to see how she would react to the tiny fur ball. Cinder had never had a litter of her own, but her maternal instincts kicked in when she licked the new pup from head to toe and even let her try to nurse. Cinder and Zoey became inseparable.

"Mama Cinder," as I called her, taught Zoey many things—so many things that Zoey's personality started to mirror that of the old girl. One of the most notable lessons was watching Cinder show Zoey the boundary of the backyard. The yard backed up on a cemetery and wasn't fenced. Cinder would take Zoey around and around the perimeter, showing her their territory. Zoey learned the lesson and never stepped outside the boundary unless I took her for a walk.

When we did walk, we'd pass through the cemetery to take a shortcut to visit a friend who lived nearby. Zoey strolled along by my side, never showing any interest in the ever-present flowers and other decorative items placed on the graves.

After having Zoey with us for nine months, the dreaded day came when I knew I had to let my old friend Cinder go. I built a box and dug a grave at the end of the backyard next to the cemetery. I left Zoey closed up in the house until I buried her "mother," Cinder, and filled in the grave.

Zoey had been watching me perform my sad chore from the window and was barking to get out. I opened the door, and she ran directly to the grave. I continued to tidy the area and noticed Zoey had disappeared. I wondered if the death was too traumatic for her. Had she become afraid and run away? She had never left the yard by herself. Would I lose this friend, too?

My worry subsided when Zoey appeared a few minutes later with a bunch of silk flowers in her mouth. She walked up slowly and placed the flowers gently on Cinder's grave. She knew. She understood.

We have taken many walks through the cemetery since that day six years ago, and Zoey has never shown any interest in the flowers. She only needed one bouquet on that particular day to honor her "mama."

Do dogs understand death? Do they have souls? Do they go to heaven? I have always believed so, but this event confirmed that all of God's creatures, humans and animals, have a soul and that we will all be reunited in heaven. My pastor once told me, "If there are no dogs in heaven, I don't want to go." I agree.

Cinder & Zoey

Farmington Pet Adoption Center
farmingtonpet.org

"The woman was terrified"

Bruce Skakle

It was a hot summer day in 2010, and my quilts were suffering from the smell of wet dogs after many joyful trips to the beach. I decided to make a trip to the nearest Laundromat in Bucksport, Maine, and take my two-year-old Golden Retriever, Ziva, with me.

After I put the quilts into the washing machine, Ziva and I headed out for a stroll along the mile-long cobblestone walkway that runs parallel to the Penobscot River. The place was packed with tourists, all enjoying the beautiful summer day.

As I was about to put Ziva's collar and leash on, she spotted a seagull on a nearby dock and must have thought it was her job to chase it off. At the same time, I saw a woman helping her child out of a car seat in a van. I watched Ziva and then looked back at the woman to see that she and a little boy were walking toward the dock. I don't know who spotted whom first, but Ziva saw that there was a kid to play with and started running toward them. The woman was terrified. She grabbed the child and picked him up. I told Ziva to stop and sit, and she dropped as if she'd been shot.

Ziva was a good girl and stayed where she was while I explained to the woman that Ziva loved kids and wouldn't hurt a fly. She told me that her five-year-old son was autistic and had never been around animals. She assured me that he would be traumatized by any contact with a dog.

I personally couldn't believe that any child could make it to five years without playing with a dog or a cat. But I assured the little boy, who didn't speak at all, that the dog was friendly and that I wouldn't let her come near him. Just as I was saying this, Ziva started crawling on her belly toward the boy. As she neared him, she rolled onto her back. I rubbed her belly, but she didn't want me. She was determined to get to the boy.

The mother watched protectively. Her son wasn't afraid but instead was waving his arms excitedly at Ziva. I noticed that the mother was speaking to him using sign language. I told her that Ziva knew sign language and could do tricks such as sit, lie down, shake hands, and high-five.

The Mom then signed, Ziva performed, and the little boy grew more and more excited. His hand started reaching out toward Ziva, and it seemed as if he wanted to touch her. So I had her turn away from him, and he touched the back of her head, pulling his hand away quickly and then touching her again. Once he did this, he waved his arms all over the place.

I then told the mom that Ziva would speak after being instructed with a hand signal and suggested that perhaps her little boy could do it. The mom made the "speak" signal, and Ziva quietly barked. The boy jumped at first and then became very excited. The mom did it again and said "speak" to Ziva, and she barked again. The mom did this four more times. I asked her if her son could try it.

The mom showed the child the "speak" sign, and after a few tries, he got Ziva to speak. What happened next was fantastic. The child, who hadn't uttered a word, made the "speak" sign, and Ziva barked. Then the little boy spoke and said, "Speak," as clear as could be. The mom looked astonished and asked me, "Did Zack say that?" She looked at me and then looked at the boy. "Did Zack say that?" she asked over and over again.

I told her he did. Then the boy signed for Ziva to speak, and again, he said, "Speak." At this point, the mom was nearly hysterical, and people were gathering to see if the dog had bitten the child. She said, "No, but my son just spoke his first word."

The next thing I knew, the mom had her cell phone out and was on the phone with her husband, who she said was an hour away. I'd never seen a person as excited as this mom. She was trying to explain to him what had happened, but it clearly wasn't registering with him. So she held the phone up near Zack and asked him to make the doggie speak. Ziva thought this was a great game to play, and she barked again. And that's when Zack said, "Speak." This time, his father heard him.

I watched as the mom excitedly spoke to her husband, and then I looked down. Zack had his arms wrapped around Ziva's neck and was hugging her for all he was worth.

When she got off the phone, the mom explained that Zack had been in speech therapy since he was eighteen months old. Other than grunts, screams, and some other sounds, he had never tried to say words. She said that experts had warned them that autistic children couldn't make emotional contact with animals. They also told her that Zack could hit or hurt an animal. So they had kept Zack away from all animals. She then told me that as soon as they got home, they would go to a shelter to look for a Golden Retriever.

After they drove away, I told Ziva she was a good girl and took her to get a vanilla kiddie cone at the ice cream shop. As usual, she was more interested in a squirrel in a nearby tree than in her cone.

I nearly didn't go to wash those smelly quilts on that beautiful summer day. What happened was divine intervention, I guess. It made my day, for sure! Ziva might be my dog, but she is a gift from God to us all.

Ziva

Bangor Humane Society
bangorhumanesociety.com

Little Bit

UnderDogs
saveunderdogs.com

"If my dog loves you, then I love you"

Sharon Murray

Little Bit was a blue-and-gold-colored, nine-pound Yorkshire Terrier who taught me more about people than I learned in the twenty-eight years of life before him. Little Bit adored me and was always by my side.

He was so devoted that when he knew I was about to have an epileptic seizure, he would bark to warn me. If there weren't any people around, he'd mimic what he'd seen others do for me during a seizure. He would wrap his little body around my neck, buffering my head and protecting it as it thrashed. He would sometimes limp for days after one of my seizures, obviously bruised. Yet it didn't prevent him from doing the same thing during the next episode.

Little Bit also protected me from people. He never bonded with my fiancé, and I never understood why until I married him. He was extremely abusive. The abuse was verbal and physical and extended to Little Bit, who was once thrown against a wall when he tried to defend me.

Eventually, I divorced the man and immediately went into another bad relationship. This time, I took my lead from Little Bit, who made his thoughts very clear. When the man spent the night, Little Bit would donate a poop inside his shoes as a nice surprise for the morning. If I left the bedroom door open, he would pee on the man's pillow and then curl up and go to sleep on mine. I got the message and ended the relationship.

When I met Donnie, I told him that if he wanted to win my heart, he would have to win the hearts of all four of my Yorkies. I explained that Little Bit would be the toughest. Donnie and I only saw each other every other Friday for a few months, and when he came over, Little Bit would greet him at the door with his tail wagging and his favorite ball in his mouth. Donnie played a lot of ball with him. And when Donnie moved in, Little Bit gave up his pillow and moved to the foot of the bed, on Donnie's side. Little Bit fell for Donnie—paws, claws, and fur. Donnie had won him over just by being himself.

Little Bit lived with Donnie and me for another five years until he died when he was nearly twenty. He died knowing I was in good hands. I am thankful that he helped me choose the right man to marry and spend the rest of my life with.

I learned from Little Bit that even though I thought I was a good judge of character, I was not. I learned to trust my animals, especially Little Bit, because I found they are able to sense the true nature of a person. To this day, I trust my dogs before I trust myself when it comes to people. Instead of "Love me, love my dog," it's "If my dog loves you, I love you."

Healing

Restoring the Balance

NickDingo

There are some dogs that come to you—not because you want or need them but because no one else wants them. They're broken and suffering. I've grown to see these dogs as gifts, given to us for a specific, character-building purpose.

I've had a few of these dogs in my life. One, in particular, was sent to teach me about patience and to help me heal.

I was working for CNN in Atlanta, producing and reporting long-format investigative stories for the network and commuting to my home in Maine, where I was based. My sister Katy, a devoted and compassionate animal rescuer, was living in Atlanta at the time. I was about to head to Maine for Christmas when Katy called to tell me she had found a dog on the Georgia 400, a twelve-lane highway. She told me he was young, an all-black Basenji mix. She said he was frightened and starving. Katy's bull's-eye was bright red, and it was on my forehead.

I was down to one dog and was enjoying the freedom of it. I pleaded with Katy to let me off the hook, but she wouldn't. No one in my family was allowed to have just one dog.

I put the dog in a crate and flew him home with me, cleverly surprising my partner, Jim, with his very own dog! He was named NickDingo, after Saint Nick and because he looked like an Australian dingo.

Every now and then, a dog comes into your life suffering from separation anxiety. In a nutshell, the dog turns into a freak the moment you leave him alone. I can tell you from experience, it isn't pretty.

I really liked my home. I loved my overstuffed, pastel-colored chairs and sofa—free of pet hair. My only "child" at the time, Philophal, a Terrier-Poodle cross, didn't shed. Life was manageable and clean.

The first time I had left the house after Nick had come onto the scene, I returned, walked into the living room, and was shocked. The whole room was awash, ankle-deep, in white fiberfill. My sofa and chairs had been murdered while I was away. I looked at Philophal, and he looked back at me with horror, saying, "I didn't do it! That dog's crazy." Finally, a scream came out of my mouth. Nick's ears flattened as he ran behind what was left of the couch.

Training ensued. Treats were involved. I dared to go to the post office for ten minutes. The couch was murdered again. This time, Nick kindly unzipped the cushions with his teeth before pulling the stuffing out.

I crated him. He bludgeoned his feet trying to get out. I put him in the cellar. Bad luck for the door. I was imprisoned in my own home with this dog I hadn't wanted. I could barely speak to my sister. I didn't have patience, and I didn't want to have it. I was a television reporter. I had to hit a deadline every day. There was no time in my life for patience.

And that's when, at thirty-two years old, I was diagnosed with a cancerous tumor in my bone marrow.

I was operated on. The doctors removed the growth, diagnosed it as a malignant bone tumor called an osteosarcoma, and advised me that I would lose my leg. Four days later, as I was prepared for a year of intensive chemotherapy, there was a miracle. The DNA results came back from the laboratory. The tumor, while presenting on slides as malignant, was in fact benign.

I was sent home to recuperate. Waiting for me was my handsome, loving boy, Philophal, and there was Nick. I was emotionally defeated and physically depleted. On top of that, the surgery had been disabling, and I had to learn how to walk again. To add one more assault to the list, my personal relationship was disintegrating. I'd had enough of life's challenges.

Nick must have understood, because he rose to the occasion, leaving behind the victim on his way to being a victor. He now had the opportunity to repay his rescue, and he took me on as a challenge. At night, he chose to sleep against my leg, providing me with his energy and warmth. And every morning, while I lay in bed wallowing in misery, Nick stood over me, nudging me with his nose. I kept my eyes closed, refusing to budge, but he wouldn't leave me alone. When nudging didn't work, he began tapping me with his foot. I'd roll over onto my stomach to get away from him. He would then stand on my back. He didn't give up until I had hobbled downstairs and emerged into the sunshine to greet the new day.

And Nick was thoughtful. He started bringing me gifts from the frozen field—something he'd made himself. We called them poop-sicles. When I refused his gifts at the door, he promptly ate them. What a guy!

Nick grew up to be a fine dog and a wonderful friend. He checked his separation anxiety at the door the moment he stopped thinking of himself to focus on me. I, in turn, stopped focusing on what I didn't have and began to see all that I did. I had faced my own mortality and realized that life was good as long as I had food, shelter, and a dog by my side. Together, Nick and I had healed.

Adam, Ma₹ie, and Adrian

Freedom Service Dogs
freedomservicedogs.org

"Life began again for me"

Freda Powell

I am the mother of twelve-year-old autistic twin boys. Adam and Adrian have had social and emotional challenges since birth. I am also a deaf parent. In October 2008, my life fell apart when Adam and Adrian's hero, my oldest son, Justin, took a job as a security guard. He was very excited. While showing off his gun to friends during a party, it discharged, killing him. He was twenty-four.

Our lives stopped. I didn't get out of bed or go outside for weeks. I shut people out and struggled every day to find myself. I wasn't alone. Adam and Adrian were having a difficult time at home and at school. I got a call every day from school complaining about their behavior. Medication wasn't helping. Therapy twice a week wasn't helping. I didn't know how to help them. We were all going through the many stages of grieving.

The thought of getting a dog crossed my mind. Before the twins were born, I had worked as a social worker and an advocate for people with disabilities. Never in a million years did I imagine I would be using the knowledge I had gained in my work with my

own children. Can you imagine twin boys with disabilities dealing with the death of their brother? It was a nightmare sometimes.
They'd have meltdowns, shutdowns, and sit on the grocery-store
floor, fold their arms in an angry gesture, and not communicate.
There were times I had to leave the food cart and carry them out
and take them home. I had tried many things over the years to help
Adam and Adrian succeed in functioning, but there weren't many
solutions to assist them mentally and socially. I had a hunch a service dog might help.

I applied to Freedom Service Dogs (FSD), a charity that rescues dogs from shelters and trains them to help people with disabilities. Six months later, we were approved for a "third-party
service dog." That meant I would be the sole handler and trainer,
because the boys weren't sixteen years old, which is the allowable
age to handle a service dog alone. Freedom Service Dogs also said
it wanted to find a match for our family, and because of that, they
didn't operate on a first-come, first-served basis. The organization
really wanted to match us with a dog that fit our lifestyle and needs,
a dog that could live in our apartment, could do well with children, could train easily, had a calm temperament, and many other
things we required and asked for. In other words, we were asking
for a perfect dog. I remember thinking to myself, "Oh, God, we're
never going to get a service dog if he has to do all these things. No
dog is that perfect!" I was wrong.

Six months later, I was introduced to a one-and-a-half-year-old
yellow Labrador Retriever named Mazie. Our training together
began immediately, every day for five hours over a period of two
weeks. It was a struggle for me at first, because I actually had to
leave the house, drive, and be in public. But the moment I saw
her, my heart took over. I began showing up early so we could

be alone. I brushed her hair and talked to her. She responded by doing everything I asked and more. The training was fun. There were forty-five commands I had to remember. Mazie sometimes did the task before I commanded it. She kept reading my mind. It was fantastic. We became a great team. During my time alone with her, I learned to relax, not just as a person but also as a mother and friend. Mazie showed me she didn't care about my baggage.

At graduation, I learned that Mazie had been dropped off at a shelter at the tender age of eight months. From there, she became part of a rehabilitation program at a women's correctional facility in Colorado, where she was trained by one of the inmates. Freedom Service Dogs then brought her into its program.

The boys didn't know how to act around Mazie at first. Adrian has a hard time bonding and showing his emotions. He stayed away from her most of the time. He refused to pet her or take her out. Adam was all over her. She slept with him most of the time. As for me, she changed my world.

Soon I was laughing so hard I was crying, skipping while walking, and sleeping better with her near me. Her presence in public is what helped me the most. She was always calm. I almost envied her. She'd feel me getting tense when people got too close and would lick my hand or bump me with her nose, giving me eye contact, letting me know she was there.

Mazie showed me acceptance by staying by me even when I was grieving and angry. She'd lay her head on my lap, lick my hand, and give me eye contact. She was compassionate when I cried. Her face would change, almost as if she was crying with me. She'd nuzzle me with her nose when I was stressed. She tolerated my habit of smoking when stressed, showed joy when I was happy by wiggling her tail and hopping around, and showed kindness when I was too tired to do anything. She somehow learned to pick up her toys and put them in her box, knowing I needed that extra help to get the chores done. It was something Justin had done as a child when I was cleaning the house after a long day at work.

More than anything, somehow this dog knew I was not myself. It was as if she could see into my soul and know that deep down, I was a loving, happy, and kind person. I didn't deserve her love. How could she love someone like me, with all the baggage, struggles, issues, and anger? I felt she must have known who I was before my son's death. That day she picked up her toys and put them in her box was the day I swore Justin was in there somewhere. She had, in fact, been born just weeks after he died.

Her intuitive ability to communicate amazed me. Ordinarily, service dogs ring a bell attached to the door to let their owners know they have to go out. Mazie somehow knew about my hearing impairment and decided to come up with her own solution. She picked up a pair of my socks and dropped them into my lap, as if to say, "Get your socks and shoes on, I have to go."

Mazie had been with us for four months. She was great with the boys, prompting them and giving them cues when they were distracted, losing time, or forgetting things. She was doing her job—ringing bells, opening doors, pulling blankets to wake the boys up, and even prompting them to behave at the dinner table. She was able to get them to do things I couldn't get them to do. It was kind of like having a second mom but better! I could now take the boys shopping with me without a meltdown.

They were focused on Mazie, who kept them from getting anxious around others. If someone got too close to them, Mazie intervened, coming to their side and making a space between them and the stranger. She was brilliant at doing her job. But even after all of this, I didn't see an emotional bond forming with Adrian. Adam and Adrian had struggled with starting relationships and maintaining them. I had hoped Mazie would help change that. I wasn't sure it was happening. Although she was doing wonders for me, I wondered if she had been a good decision for the family.

One night, my question was answered.

The boys had been playing outside. Adrian—my angry, nontrusting, withdrawn child—came inside, frustrated by the children he had been with. Adrian's been a victim of bullying since kindergarten. He was born with a partial thumb and no fingers on his right hand. He's never understood why people are mean to him. On this particular night, he came inside and described the other children as cruel and evil. He said he wanted to hurt them back. He told me he hated his life, hated everyone, and saw no good in making friends or being kind. As a mother, I was not only worried. I was scared. My child wanted to lash out and take revenge on others in order to make himself feel better. This wasn't an option!

I put Adam to bed and sat down on Adrian's bed to talk to him. I focused on his emotions and problem solving, anything to get him to stop the racing thoughts. I stayed as calm as I could, whispering so Adrian would understand that I was not angry with or disappointed in him. The first thing I said was, "I love you no matter what." He didn't believe me. I told him there were good things in life and named some great things that had happened in his life. But he was leery. So I asked him to think of one—just one—wonderful thing about his life. He whispered, "Mazie. Mazie is the most wonderful and only good thing that has happened in my life."

I realized then that Adrian and Mazie had found each other.

As Adrian and Mazie cuddled on the bed, his tummy against her back, he stroked her neck and nuzzled into her fur. I took a few steps backward toward the door to give them privacy. While he stroked her neck, I saw him say the words, "I miss you, Justin."

And there it was. He knew that this dog, like his older brother, would never think ill of him, would never be disappointed or angry with him, and would never judge him.

Adrian and Mazie fell asleep together, arms and paws entwined. As I closed the door to the bedroom that night, the tears fell. I had all but given up on the two of them, and when I least expected it, it came, on their terms, in their time, not mine.

If no human ever touches Adrian's heart, my only hope is that he will always have a Mazie in his life.

Before Mazie, I hardly ever looked beyond what I could understand as a human. I was hardly in the position to have a relationship with God after someone so close to my heart was taken from me. But now I wake up each day and know that God has sent a piece of himself and the spirit of my son through Mazie. Mazie has shown me that life can begin again.

"Perhaps you should take friendship lessons from your dog"

Theresa Pollard

I am a hard-core incest survivor. My ability to stay connected to people or animals and to follow through on relationships has always been challenging.

I was abused from the time I was a toddler. When I left home at seventeen, I was involved in the typical things the road offers: alcohol, drugs, prostitution, and violence. I had learned that adults didn't want to protect me. I grew a very cutting exterior and was rebellious and defiant against authority and most adults.

When I grew up, the shell that had long formed to protect me became impossible to crack. Relationships were often tumultuous. As soon as a relationship became questionable or uncomfortable, I would create distance, inevitably through an argument, which prevented the person from getting any closer.

Sam found me on a summer day on a beach in Del Mar, California. I was having a standoff with a lover, as was often the case. I was sitting on a rock by myself when an apparently abandoned black-and-white Springer Spaniel with no collar plopped his exhausted body down between my legs.

At that moment, I saw his innocence and vulnerability and made a decision that would change my life forever. This dog was going to be able to count on me for the rest of his life.

Sam quickly became known as the peacemaker in my life. Whenever my partner and I were in an argument, we agreed that whoever Sam went to and sat beside would get the final say. He was the mediator. The game became a way to move on and have peace.

When the relationship ended, my real lessons with Sam began.

Sam and Theresa

Gabriel's Angels: Pets Helping Kids
gabrielsangels.org

I found that our connection was built on trust, and this brought me an incredible sense of balance. I was actually having a successful relationship with someone, not running away or turning my back on him. Sam was healing me.

We camped a lot, in Yosemite and the Redwoods. Watching his freedom to be "just a dog" gave me great insight. He gave me the ability to feel more comfortable in my own skin without putting too much pressure on trying to figure out who I was. He could just be a dog, and he showed me that it was okay for me to just be a human.

I remember a stranger saying to me, "Your dog is so friendly, perhaps you should take friendship lessons from your dog." I growled under my breath. The truth was, I *was* taking lessons from my dog.

I still have problems counting on and dealing with people. But Sam taught me that it's okay to be me. He brought me peace.

"You should put other people first if you love them"

Stephanie Carlino

It was just before Christmas, and my twenty-eight-year-old daughter, Dariella, gave me a gift certificate to get a family portrait. At the time, I thought this was funny, because I have been a single parent, and she's an only child, so any picture we have of the two of us is a "family portrait."

With our two dogs in tow, we went to the photo studio. It was the usual pre-Christmas holiday madness at our local mall. There were children and frenzied shoppers everywhere. Newman, our Mini Yorkie, and Phoebe, our Mini Long-Haired Dachshund, took it all in stride.

We were propped in front of the camera by a young female photographer. It was a package deal, so we got a number of poses, and the photographer wanted each one set up a certain way. She sat us, moved us, and posed us before jumping behind the camera to take her shot. It was all very frustrating for me, as I was not as flexible as my daughter. On the fourth pose, where I was told to bend in a way I just couldn't, I stood up and announced I was done. I walked away and told them to take the remaining pictures of the dogs.

The dogs were dressed up in fairy wings and hats and put in front of a Christmas tree. I stood back and watched as the photographer did to them what she had done to me, posing and moving them around. I was glad it wasn't me. And then, as I watched, I realized they had expressions on their faces, calm expressions. They were calm and tolerant. They were doing something because someone they loved asked them to do it.

My daughter wanted a picture of us. I should have been gracious enough to sit through the session to please her, if for no other reason. Even the dogs knew that.

From my two little dogs, I learned that you should put other people first if you love them, regardless of your own feelings. I look at things differently since this happened. I know that if you do things for others, it comes back tenfold. I keep a picture of my two dogs dressed like fairies to remind me of the day I learned one of life's great lessons.

Pet Peeves
petpeevesinc.org

"I couldn't leave him behind"

Lisa MacLeod

I had just moved away from home to attend seminary school to become an ordained minister. My brindle-colored Boxer–Pit Bull, Hector, came with me. Hector was always playful and happy. I, on the other hand, was not. I'd suffered from depression my whole life. At the time of the move, my father had just passed away, and I had yet to deal with my feelings of loss. I was sinking.

Hector was my constant companion. No matter where I was in our new apartment, he was with me. We were connected in a very special way. It was as if we shared part of our souls.

Eventually, my depression overwhelmed me. And on one particular day, everything changed. I remember meeting with my therapist in the morning. She was so concerned that she sent me to the hospital. I was interviewed by staff there and then released.

My boyfriend was living in another state, and I couldn't reach him by using my calling card. We were having problems. I seemed to be having problems with everyone. I felt helpless and hopeless. I couldn't do anything right. In the evening, I went to a friend's house to use her phone. I managed to talk to my boyfriend, and the conversation didn't go well. It triggered a breakdown. I stormed out of my friend's apartment, screaming and crying uncontrollably. I headed to my own apartment to cut my wrists so I could die.

As I approached my building, I looked up to the second floor and saw Hector looking down at me from the bedroom window. He was standing with his paws on the windowsill. I looked at his face. There was fear in his eyes. At that moment, I knew I couldn't go through with it. In his face, I saw that he was concerned for me and not himself. In Hector, I saw God and heard him say to me, "I love you and care for you just as you are. On this earth, there is one who needs you still, Hector." God was reaching me through the one being I would listen to that night—the one who had never questioned or doubted me or my love.

I turned away from my apartment with one thought. I couldn't do this to Hector. I couldn't leave him behind.

I collapsed on the lawn, crying. Fortunately, my girlfriend had followed me home and came to my side. She took me to the hospital, and Hector was taken to a kennel. When I was released several days later, the one I wanted to see above everyone else was Hector. He was the one who had shown me the true meaning of unconditional love.

After this experience, I began to heal and now live with a joy for life that I've never known before. Hector has passed, but I do believe one day we'll be together again.

I'll never forget the lesson I learned that day: God speaks through all his creation, even through the loving and loyal eyes of a dog.

Friends of Kindred Spirits
friendsofks.org

Damona

Save Our Siberians Siberspace Rescue Fund
sos-srf.org

"He actually smiled"

Robert Baker

I'm a volunteer for a nonprofit organization called Tails of the Tundra Siberian Husky Rescue. We're a bunch of Husky lovers. When Huskies are in danger of being euthanized at pounds or shelters, we pull them to safety. We also take in dogs whose owners are forced to give them up because of foreclosures or other sad situations. Once the dog is safely in our care, we work to find the perfect home. I've been rescuing Huskies for ten years. I've met a lot of great dogs. But there's one I'll never forget.

Damona's rescue began on Valentine's Day, 2004, when her owners turned her over to a shelter. They said she had housebreaking issues and gave no other reason for her surrender. She was seven years old.

Tails of the Tundra pulled Damona from the shelter and temporarily placed her in one of our foster homes. In foster care, it was clear that she was housebroken but had to go out often. She did give signals when she needed to go. It was also very clear that she was a loving and affectionate dog. She showered everyone with kisses and loved to snuggle.

On two different occasions, Damona was adopted. Both times, she came back to us because she had gone to the bathroom in the house. And then, a year after we rescued her, Damona struck gold when a retiree named Joe Ferruchia adopted her. Because of his age, Joe preferred an older dog and fell in love with Damona. He followed the instructions given to him on housebreaking, and it wasn't long before Damona was free and clear of the issues that had her bouncing from home to home.

Joe and Damona lived together happily. He treated her like a princess. He discovered she was diabetic and gave her two insulin shots a day. Later, after she was diagnosed with cataracts, he paid for an expensive surgery to help her keep her eyesight.

After three great years together, Joe received bad news. He had terminal cancer.

Joe was worried about Damona and what would happen to her. We promised to help. When Joe entered a hospice facility, I brought Damona home to live with my family, including my two Siberian Huskies, Shadow and Timber. A few days later, Joe passed away. Damona was now eleven years old.

Seven months later, Tails of the Tundra was invited to speak to a fourth-grade class in Yardley, Pennsylvania, that was studying the Iditarod. Damona and I went along with another volunteer family and their dog. After I finished speaking to the students, we were invited to visit a class of autistic children.

As we walked into the room, I took note of the surroundings. The room was the size of any other elementary-school classroom. There were three teachers and fifteen kids ranging in age from six to sixteen. There was one little boy, perhaps six or seven years old, who was sitting on a chair alone in the corner of the room. When I noticed him, one of the teachers explained that he was severely autistic and rarely moved from his chair or spoke to anyone. I was told he liked to observe.

I moved to the center of the room and began talking about Damona. I explained that she was a Siberian Husky and mentioned that Huskies were sled dogs. As I spoke, the little boy who was sitting in the corner of the room stood up and walked over to me, surprising everyone.

"What's your name?" he asked.

"I'm Bob, and this is Damona," I replied.

The boy bent down and reached for her. As he did, Damona raised her nose and licked his hand. He actually smiled and placed his hand on her head. I was stunned. I handed him her leash, to see what he would do. What happened next amazed everyone. The boy held the leash loosely and began walking around the circle of children, stopping at each one. Damona followed him without being led. "This is Damona," he said, introducing each child to the dog. Damona, in return, greeted each with licks and wags. When the boy finished introducing Damona to everyone, he brought her back to me, handed me her leash, said, "Thank you," and returned to his chair.

I was in tears. It was as if, all of a sudden, I had an insight. For the first time in my life, I related to an autistic child on an intelligent level. When I saw the interaction between Damona and this child, I knew I was witnessing something very special. The teachers, too, watched in disbelief, saying they had never seen this boy interact with anyone like this. At that moment, as we all stood there, profoundly moved by what had just happened, I knew that this special dog—this dog who had been thrown away so many times—had just made a big difference in a little boy's life.

What I didn't know then was that Damona was about to shed her grace on yet another family. She had been with us for a year when a family who had adopted one of our Huskies four years earlier told us they were looking for a companion for him. They were specific. They wanted an older, "laid-back" female.

I delivered Damona to their home a week later. The next day, I received a call from the family, reporting in with a great story. They explained that every night, their dog, Brahms, slept on a bed near their bed. Every morning, they would take his bed and put it under their bed. And every night, he would pull his bed out from underneath theirs and fall asleep on it, never moving again until morning.

On Damona's first night, Brahms pulled his bed out and went to sleep. But when they woke the next morning, Brahms had moved and was sleeping back-to-back with Damona.

Damona touched a great many lives, both human and canine, during her all-too-brief time here on earth. It would not be an exaggeration to say she was a divine dog. I am grateful to have been given the opportunity to be part of her life.

Footnote: After only a year with Brahms and his family, Damona died of kidney failure. I am certain her former owner, Joe, was waiting to greet her when she passed and that their reunion was joyful.

"They fell to the floor together"

Marilyn Tyma

When I was a graduate student in counseling psychology, I chose to do my internship at an alternative school. The director was willing to let me use my dog in counseling sessions, and for me, that was a dream come true.

Bruin was a black Giant Schnauzer who loved to ride in the car with his head sticking out through the sunroof with his Doggles on. He was funny, intelligent, independent, and very sensitive. He had a beautiful ability to know when someone was hurting.

One day at school, a twelve-year-old boy named Steve came into the counseling program. He'd been in foster care and institutions his entire life. He was suffering from physical, mental, and emotional abuse. As a result, he didn't look at or speak to anyone. We had several noncommunicative sessions. Then, one day, we had a breakthrough. We were in a private room. Bruin was with us. Bruin and I sat on the floor across from Steve, who chose to lie on the floor curled up in his usual fetal position, something not unusual given his history. Bruin got up and went over to Steve and lay

down next to him. He then put his paw on Steve's leg. It startled
Steve at first, and he looked to me for direction. I told him that
Bruin just wanted to be near him. Steve looked at Bruin, smiled,
and gently began petting his head.

A few minutes later, Steve began talking to Bruin. I was
stunned. For the next several sessions Steve spoke with me a little
bit but mainly talked to Bruin. His body changed—he was no longer in a fetal position. He sat up and talked and was more inter-
active. At the beginning of each session, Steve entered the room
calling Bruin's name as he greeted him. Two weeks after our sessions began, Steve started speaking to people but never the way he
spoke to Bruin. He trusted Bruin.

When Steve left the program, he came to me and asked if he
could give Bruin a hug good-bye. He then asked permission to give
Bruin a gift. I said it would be okay if he really wanted to. And then
I watched as the young boy pulled his only possession out of his
pocket, a rawhide bracelet with four plastic beads on it. He tied it to
Bruin's collar. He said it was so that Bruin would never forget him.

My internship at the school ended, and I took a full-time position there as a counselor. Three years passed. Bruin had grown
tired and arthritic, and I started working with a new dog. But on
one special day, I decided to take Bruin to school with me. I knew
it would be his last time. He could hardly walk anymore, but he
wanted to go. It broke my heart to leave him home alone, so I decided to take him on that final day.

I had left Bruin in a counseling room and was walking down the
hallway when a tall boy grabbed my arm and said, "Hey, you're the
dog lady! Where's Bruin?" It was Steve. I barely recognized him.
He had shot up at least a foot in height. He told me he was inter-
viewing to reenter the school and asked if he could see Bruin. I led

him by the arm to the counseling room. Steve ran to Bruin, who recognized Steve and tried to jump on him. They fell to the floor together and snuggled. Bruin howled with happiness, and Steve cried. Bruin was still wearing the piece of rawhide around his collar that Steve had given him three years before.

Bruin passed away a few days later. I still have his collar with that very symbolic bracelet hanging from it.

Dogs have the ability to open doors that others can't. I'm a much better counselor when I have my co-counselor with me.

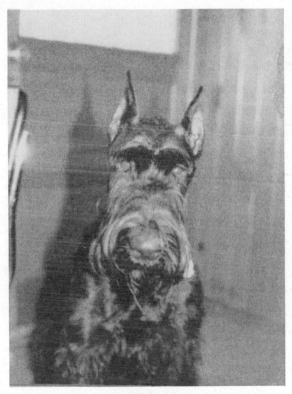

Bruin

Giant Schnauzer Rescue
ht-z.org

"He's our blessing"

Carol Bradshaw

My husband, Jack, is a veteran of the Vietnam War and suffers from posttraumatic stress disorder (PTSD). There was no one incident that brought on the PTSD but a series of horrific events that led to it.

Jack watched fellow soldiers die, picked up body parts after skirmishes, and saw a young medic blown up by a land mine. He was often on the run and fighting for his life. There was never any rest. When he wasn't on a mission, one of his jobs at headquarters included unloading bodies from Huey helicopters and then cleaning up the blood to prepare the chopper for its next flight.

Did Jack see or experience anything different from any other soldier? Probably not. But what he saw and experienced affected the rest of his life.

Anger issues, distrust of authority, hypervigilance, depression, and panic attacks are all symptoms of PTSD. When Jack was younger, he was able to cope with all of these issues to a certain extent, but as he got older, the disorder reared its ugly head every day. In 2004, the PTSD took its toll. Jack was fifty-seven and physically beaten up from working as a roofer for almost forty years. He was worried about everything and was always waiting for something bad to happen. He was depressed and anxious and was becoming reclusive, even from friends and family. That's when he put a gun to his head. I was able to talk him out of killing himself and got him to the closest veterans hospital, in Loma Linda, California. With counseling, group meetings, wonderful doctors, and medication, he was able to move forward again.

We don't have any children. Animals have always been members of our family. One day, a veteran friend told us a sad story about a big black dog named Bandit who needed a permanent home. We were told he had been given away, time and again, only to run back to the home he loved. But his owner couldn't keep him. Each time he ran back to her, he was bruised, battered, and suffering. After hearing his story, we went to meet Bandit. His big brown eyes melted our hearts. We took him on the condition that he got along with our three cats. It wasn't a problem. He fit into our home the moment he stepped through the door. Little did we know then that by providing a permanent home for him, he would bring comfort and peace into our lives.

Jack experiences periods of hypervigilance during the night. We call it "walking the perimeter." It's when Jack gets out of bed and walks around the house and the backyard, checking for the enemy. Bandit had been with us for six months when I noticed something extraordinary. Jack wasn't walking the perimeter as much as he had before. He seemed to be sleeping more restfully and for longer periods of time. At the same time, I noticed that Bandit would get up several times during the night and walk throughout the house and then come back to the bedroom, to his bed on the floor next to Jack. It appeared that Bandit was now walking the perimeter and that Jack, while sleeping, was unconsciously aware of it and was resting easier. It was as if Bandit took over the duty of protecting the family and was allowing Jack to sleep.

All was going well until Jack experienced a trigger event that brought the bad memories rushing back again. He was driving on a freeway when a dog wandered into the road. The dog was hit by a car and literally exploded into pieces in front of him. Within days of witnessing the accident, Jack was back in the hospital. It was there that he was visited by a therapy dog named Riley. Riley, a Corgi mixed breed, became the catalyst for a turning point in our life.

Knowing what Bandit was already doing for Jack and seeing the response that Jack had to Riley, we decided to see if Bandit might qualify as a therapy dog. At the time, we thought it would be our way of giving back to other veterans. Bandit passed the course with flying colors and immediately started working with cancer, dementia, and psychiatric patients at the VA hospital.

While Bandit was helping others with their health issues, we noticed that he was involved in making dramatic changes at our home. Bandit now had Jack's back. He had his eyes constantly on him, reading his moods and thoughts. It was as if helping Jack was his job.

He now intercepted people who got too close to Jack, moving his body to act as a barrier between them. And when Jack needed to climb stairs, Bandit went up with him, slowly taking each step while keeping his body in a bracing stance, helping Jack keep his balance. Bandit was the support system Jack had never had.

We were told that Bandit could go a step further and train to be a California assistance dog. The training would allow Bandit to accompany Jack anywhere. More important, Bandit would learn how to recognize oncoming depression and panic attacks and work to prevent them. Once again, Bandit passed the training. And once again, our lives soared to a new height.

Since Bandit came into our lives, Jack is more independent and is able to do normal things again. Bandit's presence has prevented Jack from falling into the black hole that he can drop into. When he starts to head toward depression and anxiety, Bandit knows and nudges him, alerting him that he's going into a place he doesn't have to go. And with Jack's increasingly difficult mobility issues, he's able to count on Bandit as a "brace" dog.

Bandit has been a member of our family for four years. He thrives on helping Jack and loves volunteering with other veterans. His name was Bandit when we got him. We figure it's because he steals hearts. He's our blessing.

Jack and Bandit

Helping Every Animal League
friendsofheal.org

Guinness

Therapy Dogs International
tdi-dog.org

"Love is patient"

Patrick Klingaman

L ove is patient" is a famous quote from the Bible. Despite my familiarity with the principle, I haven't always demonstrated great levels of patience with others, and certainly not with myself.

From an early age, I had a strong, self-generated sense of ambition. Between the age of ten and twelve, I remember pointing to the bookcase of encyclopedias and informing my mother that I would be in there someday. From success gurus, I learned to set measurable goals. For decades, I set dozens of annual goals and tracked my progress in activities such as writing, reading, and even praying. But when I fell short of my goals, I often felt I wasn't measuring up.

As I grew older, I looked back on my career as a marketing director and thought of my lack of patience with others. I had always seen myself as an agent of change. When other executives failed to see what I saw, I often felt angry and frustrated.

When I reached forty-eight, I found myself battling a back-muscle injury. It was so painful that when I bent down to pull on my boots, the muscle pain and spasms literally had me on the floor. I spent much of the year visiting specialists and in physical therapy,

135

with frequent reinjuries and only partial healing. I gained fifteen pounds, and my cholesterol skyrocketed, substantially increasing my risk of a heart attack.

Guinness, a joy-filled black Portuguese Water Dog, came into my life when I needed her most. She was a puppy who soon grew into a sixty-pound dog. Before Guinness, I had always had lap dogs that required minimal activity. Guinness was different. She was a working dog. She was bored in obedience class and failed her first test toward becoming a therapy dog. I quickly found that she had minimal retrieving skills on land and none in the water. But Guinness needed something to do.

With chronic health issues and career setbacks, I had settled into a middle-age rut. I wasn't depressed or suicidal, but I had little to be excited about. I decided to try agility, hoping the exercise would be good for me and for Guinness.

Dog agility is a sport in which a handler must accurately direct a dog through an obstacle course in a race against time. It's a competition. Once I started running agility with Guinness, her boundless enthusiasm was contagious.

That first agility run was a misadventure, more entertaining but just as chaotic as a train wreck. So, too, were ninety-nine of our first one hundred runs. Ah, but that other run. I was the apprehensive handler, with my barking black shadow springing through a maze like a movie chase scene that everyone expects will end in a crash. Not this time. At the final jump—our finish line—she bounded to me to receive her well-deserved treat. Her open mouth and protruding tongue complemented an intensely excited stare, rarely seen except when she was wet. Guinness wasn't the only one coming alive again. We had finally found an activity that we were equally excited about doing together.

The sound of ripping Velcro as I adjusted a brace was Guinness's cue that we were going to train. And while my runs with her lasted less than a minute, they briefly transported me to a place free of physical limitations, where I could experience the simple joys of a boy and his dog. My doctor confirmed what I'd been feeling. After a year of agility classes together, my health had improved dramatically. I had cut my risk of a heart attack in half. My cholesterol had dropped to a record low of 151 (from 293), and all of the other higher-risk measurements were now in the low-risk range.

Two years after my first class, I began to see signs that the lessons of my new pastime might be deeper than originally thought. For example, training animals for a complex performance event is a case study in patience. Despite many months of efforts that were more blooper reel than blue-ribbon material, I rarely experienced impatience. Was it because of the look of total devotion as Guinness scrambled to follow my lead? Or was it her unfailing enthusiasm and the glimpse of potential I saw even in a disastrous run? Or maybe it was the fact that our rare feats of greatness brought me so much pleasure that I would replay the run over and over in my head and forget the rest.

One day, I finally made the connection. If I, as a rookie handler, never considered giving up on my dog, why would I ever think that God would give up on me? God, more than anyone, knows my true potential, something I'm still discovering through life's trials and errors. If one shining moment can eclipse a mountain of miscues on an agility course, I imagine that the joy is vastly greater in God's case.

Guinness's expression of joyful excitement while running sustained me through the years of classes, practices, and competitions, eventually allowing me to help her become the champion I always knew she was. When we're in sync, barreling through an agility course, I feel fully alive. That enthusiasm overflows into the rest of my life. Guinness has brought me back to health, physically, emotionally, and spiritually.

I didn't always demonstrate great levels of patience with others or with myself. My breakthrough came from neither sermon nor book but from the depths of a working relationship with my dog. Some people discover lessons about life and themselves through participation in grand undertakings. But for most of us, revelation can be found in the midst of more basic pursuits. I run with dogs. I'm not sure that I'll ever feel accomplished at that endeavor, but I will always marvel at what the endeavor has accomplished in me.

"Kindness never goes unrecognized"

Dion Genovese

This story is about a gentle giant known as Hemingway and his journey in helping to heal others. I met Hemingway, a brindle-colored Bull Mastiff–Rotweiler mix, at the Ashton Animal Clinic in Sarasota, Florida, where I work as a receptionist. The one hundred thirty-pound dog had been brought in by animal services to be neutered. He was a kind soul with large brown eyes.

Dr. Laurie Walmsley, the owner of the clinic, was looking for a dog to fill a spot in her heart that was left when her beloved Rottweiler, Barnacle Bill, died six months before. She called animal control to inquire about adopting the big Mastiff-Rottie but was told he'd already been adopted.

A week later, Dr. Laurie came into the clinic to see the big boy sitting in a kennel staring at her. The family who'd adopted him had given him up. He was too big for their condominium. It was meant to be. Dr. Laurie named him Hemingway because the way he moved with continuous love and compassion was like witnessing poetry in motion. That day, all of our lives changed forever.

Hemingway quickly became the mayor of Ashton Clinic. He watched each day as Dr. Laurie treated animals and performed surgeries and always greeted anyone who walked through the doors with a genuine smile. He also had a way of pushing himself through your legs, often lifting you off the floor as a way of saying hello.

Hemingway's rounds involved visiting the in-house boarders and also the hospitalized cats and fellow canines. He was a celestial presence from another world who provided comfort to all the animals. After making his rounds by checking on the patients, he'd free-roam the clinic halls, often visiting me at the desk and greeting clients as they arrived. He had a way of saying to everyone, "Your worries stop here."

One day, I watched as Hemingway made his way to the waiting room to find a client in tears. He walked over to her and rested his giant head on her lap. As she stroked his head, she cried and explained that she had terminal cancer and little time. The woman had brought her dog in for one last check before she died. Hemingway knew she needed comforting, and for a brief time, she felt his love. He understood.

It was clear that Hemingway had a gift with people, but we quickly learned that his gifts extended to helping other dogs. It started with an emergency. A dog came in with a rattlesnake bite. Because of the venom, the dog's blood couldn't clot. He needed a blood transfusion. But who would give the blood? Hemingway came forward and sat quietly as his blood was collected. The blood transfusion provided life-saving platelets and healthy red blood cells to control the dog's bleeding and enabled us to continue to treat the toxicity from the snakebite. Hemingway saved his life.

Pretty soon, whenever one of Dr. Laurie's patients needed blood, Hemingway gave the gift. He saved one dog with parvovi-

rus, another suffering from a splenic tumor, and another with au-
toimmune hemolytic anemia. Hemingway's reputation for giving
blood became well known. Before long, the local veterinary oncologist called on him to help her patients. He never stopped giving.

Hemingway started out as an unwanted stray, homeless and
abandoned. Someone overlooked his many gifts. In this case, one
man's loss was another man's and many dogs' gain.

Hemingway was one of the kindest, gentlest, most giving souls
I have ever met. He was a celestial being, in tune to every person
and animal he came in contact with. He truly seemed to be from
another world in his ability to provide comfort just with his presence. Through Hemingway, I became aware that being sensitive to
others' pain and reaching out with kindness never go unrecognized
or unrewarded.

Dr. Laurie and Hemingway

Animal Rescue Coalition
animalrescuecoalition.org

Walter J. Fox and Jayne

Boston Terrier Rescue Net
bostonrescue.net

"Praise for the heathen who abandoned him"

Jayne Fagan

I moved from the East Coast to the West Coast to be around college friends and escape a "spin cycle" relationship—the type where you don't know up from down because it's just so crazy and abusive. I had been adjusting to this new life for a few months when I placed an application with a rescue group that specialized in Boston Terriers. The criteria for my new dog was simple and could be summed up in three words: female, puppy, cute.

At the time, I was working as a waitress at a pub that had a "no cell-phone use" policy during work. One day, when my shift was over, I noticed I had missed a phone call from the dog rescue lady. I called her back, and she told me I was too late. She was on her way to drop the dog off with another applicant. I had missed the dog of my dreams, a sweet little peanut of a dog, by twenty minutes. I would have named her Ruby or Susan, perhaps. But I missed the call, and the crazy dog lady gave her to someone else. Little did I know, greater things were in store for me.

It was a chilly Friday evening when I got the next call. The vibrant, borderline-obnoxious rescue lady had a little man for me. He had been left at a dentist office in Salem, Oregon. Someone had opened the door and shoved his overstuffed body into the waiting room. Praise for the heathen who abandoned him. He knew the dentist was a dog lover and wouldn't toss his sorry-looking butt onto the street.

But there were complications. I didn't want a boy dog, and I was told he was old and had "fat sacks" on his tummy. Really? What was a fat sack? I had to meet this beast. I was intrigued.

The rescue lady brought him to me. I gave her one hundred dollars, a discount because of his fatty tumors, and took him "on hold" for the week, just in case I wanted to give him back. He was a lumpy black-and-white-spotted Boston Terrier–French Bulldog mix. I was hesitant.

The moment we walked into my house, the yet-unnamed man started humping my roommate's black Labrador. Some call that establishing dominance. I call it why I didn't want a boy dog.

Twenty minutes later, the boy had settled in, and boy, could he snore—worse than my eighty-five-year-old gramps. It was an insane, gut-wrenching type of snoring. Visions of sleep apnea and the costs of a breathing machine ran through my brain. That first night, I sat in awe, watching the he-beast slurping while he snored away at the foot of the couch. With that face, much like that of the great Walter Matthau, I could not help but fall in love with him. From that moment onward, I knew I was in it for the long haul. I would love this lumpy bastard and prance him around the snooty dog parks with pride. I would make him wear a poncho in the rain and dress him like a ladybug for Halloween. He would ride in the basket of my vintage bike to pleasure-cruise and save his old, tired legs. Alas, like a fool, I fell for him—and I fell hard.

I named him Walter J. Fox, after Walter Matthau, because he looked like him, and Michael J. Fox, because he had personality and spirit. Not to sound like a sappy Lifetime movie, but this pup really helped me get back to myself. Before my bad relationship, I had been very social. My friends considered me to be funny and entertaining. I loved to joke around. But I had lost my light. Walter came to me toward the end of a dark period, when I was adrift. And with him, I immediately had someone who loved me. On the good days, he was there to stampede wildly through parks with me or to go on camping trips. On the bad days, he would cuddle next to me under the covers while I cried. As I was healing, he was my constant companion.

There were many things about Walter that I loved. When it rained, he had an air about him as he entered the dog park in a yellow rain slicker, feeling it but not showing the shame. And he didn't show any shame on taco night, either. He loved tacos so much that my roommates and I decided he was a refugee from Tijuana who was smuggled across the border in a burrito truck. Walter J. Fox loved to lick feet, cuddle, and snore like a banshee. He loved dog parks, the occasional game of fetch, roaming the woods, and sitting shotgun in the car.

When people asked me about him, I told them I decided to keep him because he was so damned old and ugly that no one else would cart his lumpy butt around in a bicycle basket. In honesty, he had my heart.

As our days turned into months together, I found my silly self again. And there had been other changes in me. I found that I was less inclined to care about appearances and "how things should be." Walter taught me not to stress about things and to go with the flow. He showed me that I didn't have to do a billion things at once.

Sometimes I just needed to enjoy a cuddle. Walter J. Fox reminded me that I was loved, no matter what.

A friend once told me that God brings certain people into your life at a time when you need them. I believe that. I wanted and needed the dog of my dreams, and that's exactly who I got.

Gratitude

Appreciating Home

Sadie & Philophal

I once rescued a dog. I bestowed upon her one kindness. Her gratitude lasted a lifetime.

I was working as an investigative environmental correspondent for CNN in Atlanta when I was given an assignment in Puerto Rico. My job was to investigate the movement by U.S. companies to set up factories on the island in order to fly under the radar of federal environmental guidelines imposed on them in the United States. Some businesses were dumping toxic waste into the rivers and streams on the island, contaminating entire communities. I was also there to do a story about Puerto Rico's El Yunque Rainforest, the only tropical forest in the U.S. National Forest System.

I was scheduled to spend five days on the island covering the stories. The first day, my crew and I were booked to shoot the rainforest, forty kilometers southeast of the capital of San Juan. As we approached the base of the magnificent Luquillo Mountains, my photographer stopped to take some shots. I got out of the car and looked around. There was trash strewn everywhere—everything from beds and appliances to household rubbish. It was a dumping ground. Apparently, the U.S. companies weren't the only ones trashing the island.

I thought of the contrast between the beauty of the rainforest above us and the beast of human waste strewn across the base of one of the most beautiful places in the world. I asked my photographer to take some shots of the garbage. I would be including it in my story. He agreed with me and turned his lens away from the mountain.

A moment later, he yelled out, "Take a look at this!" I walked over. His lens was focused on a box that appeared alive. I stepped up and looked closer. Maggots. There were millions of swarming white maggots in the box. And they had formed the outline of a dead dog and its puppies.

I walked away. And that's when the photographer called out again, "You're not going to believe this." One of the puppies was alive and outside the box. I walked back, and as I did, the pup, perhaps eight weeks old, crawled toward me using only its two front paws, its back legs dragging behind.

It was heartbreaking. Everyone on the crew let out a different expletive at the same time. I ran back to the van and collected a sandwich and a bottle of water. I pulled the meat out of the sandwich and gave it to the puppy, who devoured it. I then cupped my hand and filled it with water. Again, the puppy drank. Afterward, the tiny survivor looked up at me with the most grateful eyes.

A moment later, the crew finished shooting and called for me. I was sternly told to leave the dog behind—we were on a tight schedule, and there was nothing I could do for it.

It was one of those critical moments in my life, a moment that defined who I was. I got into the backseat of the van, and we headed for the mountains. No one said anything until the head popped out of my bag.

"You can't bring that dog!" the photographer barked. "We have to climb a mountain. And you can't leave it in a hot car."

"I couldn't leave it there!" I said. "We'll figure it out."

And we did figure it out, that dog and I. We climbed a mountain together, shared lunch, finished the shoot, and snuck into a four-star hotel when we got back to San Juan. That night, I gave the dog a bath and fell asleep with her curled under my chin.

Over the next few days, the dog was boarded at a veterinarian's, where she was vaccinated while I tried to "sell" her to all the good people of Puerto Rico who were hosting parties in our honor and acting as our guides. But unbeknownst to me, Puerto Rico had a severe pet overpopulation problem. There was no home on the island for this puppy.

To make a long story short, the little dog took a long flight home with me, and I promptly gave her to my brother Billy, who had been hoping to get a dog. He named her Sadie, and from that day onward, she was known as Sadie the Puerto Rican Lady.

A week later, I called my brother to see if he was itching. He said he wasn't, but his girlfriend was. I had to give them the bad news. Sadie had given me scabies, and they needed to be treated for the parasite, too. The bugs had burrowed under my skin and were moving around, causing extreme itchiness and discomfort. It was really gross.

Billy and I lived in different parts of the country, and we saw each other about once a year. The first time I saw Sadie after her rescue was a year later. Sadie had grown up to be a white-and-tan wire-haired dog the size of a Jack Russell. She was healthy, and all four legs were nourished and working. As I walked up the path toward my brother's apartment, he opened the door, and Sadie ran toward me with unspeakable joy. I lifted her up, and she licked me enthusiastically. She couldn't control her excitement. I sat down on the grass, and she ran around me in circles and then ran up my back and jumped off, repeatedly. No one in my life had ever been that happy to see me.

Every year after that, for the rest of her life, I made a point of visiting Sadie. And every time I saw her, even when she was an old girl, she gave me the same reception.

Throughout my life, I've heard it said that dogs don't have memories or feelings. I've even heard people surmise that animals don't feel pain. Many of these myths have come from scientists who don't believe in anthropomorphism. They don't believe animals can have human qualities such as empathy and gratitude. These statements have come from scientists who, I feel, have rejected anthropomorphism in order to justify their own experimentation on animals. Today, that's changing, because every one of us who has lived the true "life experiment" with a dog, and that includes many scientists, knows better.

Sadie the Puerto Rican Lady loved me from the moment I whisked her away from certain death and was always grateful to me. From my experience with her, I learned that you should do what you know is right even if you have to go against others. I feel that I have accomplished a lot in my life. Rescuing Sadie was one of my greatest achievements.

"No whining, no hurt feelings, no bitterness"

Lee Gaitan

It is a blustery twenty-eight degrees in the wee hours of a wet January morning. I cut quite a figure standing in my front yard— red flannel nightgown, white socks and brown loafers, topped with an ill-fitting rain slicker left over from sometime before the dawn of disco. Icy pellets sting my face. Gusting winds whip my nightgown like a single-ply Kleenex. I am shivering, wet, and half-asleep. My warm bed coos seductively, yet I stay firmly planted, braving the elements. What could prompt such behavior in a grown woman? Temporary insanity? A full lunar eclipse? Prescription drugs? Nope, something even stronger and more compelling: love. Puppy love, to be more specific.

I am standing outside in the near dead of night because fourteen pounds of puppy pulled me from my slumber, deceived me into thinking he meant business, and, now that he's here, committed only to sniffing every square inch of the lawn. He has total disregard for my comfort and shows not a whit of remorse. And the only way I could be more in love with him is if he learned to talk and said to me, "Pardon my saying so, but I think you could stand to put on a little weight."

Six weeks ago, love came to my house, and I'm learning anew at forty-two the truth that love can soothe what love has burned and burned badly. Six months before, I had hit the trifecta. I was caring for a sister with Parkinson's disease, my husband was downsized out of a job, and I had to make the wrenching decision to put my beloved eleven-year-old Springer Spaniel, Ruckus, to sleep. She

Jif

Friends to the Forlorn Pit Bull Rescue
friendstotheforlorn.com

was my baby, my buddy, my comfort blanket, and my comic relief. I ached for her deep in my heart, in my soul, and in my bones. I missed her in big ways (no knock-over greetings at the door) and in small ways (no gentle snoring in the corner of my bedroom). Finally, and with great reluctance, I started the motions of "moving on." Dog beds and bowls were gathered up. Half-chewed toys and bones were tossed out. Collar and leash were neatly tucked away in a keepsake box.

Gradually, sniffling at dog-food commercials gave way to laying big plans for living a new life, dog-free. I imagined the frontiers I could conquer now that I wasn't tied down to a dog. I could stay out all day, all night, even, with no pet to answer to or worry about. There would be no water bowls to fill, no walks to take or baths to give. And the savings in vet bills alone would enable me to take an early retirement. I would have total freedom. My friends sighed with envy. I agreed with slightly feigned relief. Nary a dog hair, much less a muddy paw print, would ever cross the threshold of my spiffy new car. My French doors, free at last of smeary nose prints, would sparkle in the sunshine. My carpets, freshly shampooed and scented, would stay that way for weeks now, maybe months. Yes, it was going to be so . . . so . . . clean, and quiet, and lonely.

That's when love came. I had stopped at an Office Depot for some home-office supplies when, by coincidence, I noticed that the PetSmart next door was having an adoption day. I didn't want to look, because the loss of Ruckus was too painful. Even when one of the workers held up a tiny caramel-colored fur ball, I kept insisting I was not in the market for a new dog. Finally, the worker understood and lifted the paw of the yet-unnamed Jif to wave good-bye to me. "Put him in the car," I said with happy resignation, feeling myself take the last step out of the abyss and back into the sunlight.

I named him Jif for his color but mainly because choosy mothers choose Jif. I was told he was a Labrador mix who had been found, alone and abandoned, in a Dumpster. Straight into my heart he came, with sweet, soft, soothing love. He came without papers, pedigree, or pretense, with only unabashed, unconditional puppy love to give. Okay, he also came with a wet nose, muddy paws, and a leaky plumbing system.

Order has now given way to full-blown chaos in my tidy home. Squeaky toys litter the hallways, socks and slippers are safe only when stored at ceiling height, and every ground-level pane of glass bears a distinctive smudge. I doubt if an undistinguished little mutt is quite what Proust had in mind when he wrote, "The real voyage of discovery consists not in seeking new landscapes but in having new eyes." But new eyes are exactly what this puppy has given me. It's hard not to be caught up in the sheer joy and wonder he exhibits at being alive. He is utterly convinced that the entire world and everyone in it were invented solely to respond to his greeting. He approaches everyone with the same open, expectant, "wanna play" attitude. And the funny thing is, nine times out of ten, they do. As for the ones who don't, he simply moves on; no whining, no hurt feelings, no bitterness. A life lesson on four legs if ever there was one.

Day by day, this dipsy-doodle-apple-streudel-silly-noodle of a puppy is teaching me all over again about life and love. With each lick of my face, I feel sunshine seeping into the cracks and crevices of my soul, bringing light to dark places that were marinated in sadness. My glasses may be smeared, but my vision has been renewed. And I am grateful. So the next time you see me shivering in my nightgown, trying to coax along a pokey pup—the same frightened fur ball who once whimpered alone in a dark, dirty Dumpster—I know exactly what you'll be thinking: "You lucky dog!" And indeed I am.

"He's my little guru"

Jenny Block

I never was a dog person. I've had a few in my life, and they were all very sweet, but they never "spoke" to me. Then I met Walter. He was ugly as sin, a tiny, scruffy, Chihuahua–Cairn Terrier mix, a few weeks old and weighing just a few pounds. He'd been abused something awful and did little more at the shelter than shake in the corner, wrapped around his tiny brother.

I was at the shelter to visit the kittens, but I ended up holding Walter's fragile little body for hours, nuzzling my face into his mangy fur. I managed to go home without him that night, but I slept fitfully. I wanted him desperately. The next morning, back I went.

The shelter explained that Walter had been seized with a warrant, along with thirty other animals from the same home. When I asked for details, the shelter worker said it would be better if I didn't know. As it turned out, Walter really did have mange and kennel cough and allergies and lousy kneecaps. But none of that mattered, because I could do no wrong in his eyes, even when I was a little late with his supper.

Walter has an ability to know what I need, when I need it, and that makes him divine. If I'm sick or sad or stressed, he lays his body

157

on mine and licks my face. If I'm antsy, he scratches at the door until I take him for a walk. If I'm angry, he rolls onto his back, making me forget everything else so I can rub his naked belly. Walter just knows.

A friend once commented that Walter and I are exactly alike. We have terrible seasonal allergies and skinny little legs, are very loyal, and love to be snuggled. We also need a lot of attention but enjoy our time alone.

One day, Walter did something that changed me forever. It was such a simple thing, but in an instant, I realized how profound it was. I was doing what I'm always doing: writing on my laptop, talking on my mobile, writing down notes in my journal, looking up recipes for dinner—frantic all at once. In the middle of it all, Walter hopped up onto the arm of the overstuffed chair I was in and started pawing at my face. He pawed and pawed and pawed. I finally stopped the million things I was doing to look at him. My intention was to bat him away and tell him to stop. But instead, I stopped. He looked at me, and I knew instantly what he was trying to say: "Slow down. One thing at a time. None of these things is a matter of life or death. Relax. Take a minute to scratch my head and to see how much I love you. Be present."

Every time I feel overwhelmed and removed from my own body, I think of that moment and the look in Walter's weepy eyes when he taught me one of life's most valuable lessons. Now I do my best to be present, no matter what I'm doing. I try to focus on one thing at a time. And I always remember to take the time to scratch his little head whenever he asks.

Walter has taught me so many things. Sometimes it seems as if he's my little guru. He practices yoga every morning, not because he knows what the heck it is but because he knows his little body needs to stretch before he starts his day. Downward Facing

Dog every morning and every evening. He only eats until he's full. He's wary of strangers until they've proven themselves. He always takes the time to check out everything around him, to look at it and sniff it and consider it from every angle. But the most important thing I've learned from Walter is that there's always time to love and be loved. No matter how crazy a day awaits me, he insists on snuggling in the morning, curved into my body, licking my hand. He sighs and stretches and puts his paws on me as if to say, "The day can wait a minute, and you'll be all the better for it if you spend just one minute thinking of nothing but how lucky we are to love and be loved." Maybe he's just lazy and doesn't want to wake up. But I don't think so. More than anything, Walter's taught me to stay in the moment, because, after all, moments are all we have.

The universe has a funny way of making sure you have what you need when you need it. My needs just happen to be contained in a scruffy little canine body. And for that, I couldn't be more grateful.

Walter

Society for the Prevention of Cruelty to Animals Texas

spca.org

Hooch

Senior Animal Medical Aid Fund
samafund.org

"A twist of fate"

Michele Newman-Gehrum

It was the new year in 2009 when an e-mail from a person I didn't know found its way to my in-box. It was a mass e-mail pleading for someone to step in to help an old feller named Hooch get to safety. That e-mail was a twist of fate that changed my life.

Hooch spent the first ten years of his life chained outdoors. He suffered through the blistering winters and blazing summers of upstate New York with no human contact and little food and water. Neighbors called animal control officers time and again, but their hands were tied. Hooch, after all, had a run-down, dilapidated doghouse, and because of that, his owners were protected under law. There was no law that protected Hooch from neglect.

The New York State Department of Education's office building in Utica overlooked the tan-and-brown Mastiff-Bloodhound, where he stood in his own feces, chained to one spot in a junk-laden backyard. Day after day and year after year, employees watched as he barked at passersby, pleading for help. One woman reported that she stopped opening her office blinds because she couldn't look at him anymore. For ten years, they watched. And then, one day, they noticed he wasn't coming out of his wooden structure anymore. They called the animal welfare officers again. The officers went to the owner's home and asked the people there to sign Hooch over to them. They refused.

A few days later, Hooch apparently found the strength to break the chain that tethered him. And he ran. He ran for his life. And the community, seeing him free, rallied. Animal control officers picked him up. Once he was in protective custody, with the choke chains still embedded in his neck, a local rescue group sent out appeals to help him escape. And that's when I got that e-mail.

We were having a snowstorm. But that wasn't going to stop me. My husband, Bill, and I didn't hesitate. We hopped into our car and made the four-hour trip to rescue Hooch. We picked him up at the Stephen Swan Humane Society, where a crowd had gathered to see him off. There were dozens of community members there, including Department of Education employees, people who had fed him over the years, people from other rescue groups, and more. I waited in the crowd as my husband took him by the leash. And then Hooch turned, looked directly at me, smiled, and ran to my open arms. It was as if we were long-lost friends, finally reunited. As we said good-bye, there were many tears. The woman who had shut her office blinds because she couldn't stand seeing the abuse was there, and she was sobbing. In the end, she had helped facilitate his freedom.

Hooch had physical scars on his neck, where the chains had embedded in his skin. And he had emotional scars, too—he couldn't relax and was filled with anxiety and uncertainty. He was sixty-seven pounds. He was meant to be one hundred twenty.

Night after night, Hooch couldn't sleep. He paced. When he did sleep, he'd wake in a panic. Every night in the bone-chilling cold of February in upstate New York, we walked the streets together to settle him. When we returned home, I slept on the floor with him, stroking his fur and kissing his head, reassuring him that he was safe. I promised he would never be harmed again and that he would never be cold or hungry. He absorbed all the love I bestowed upon him. I introduced him to cookies, tennis balls, and car rides. And then, one morning, after he had been with us for five weeks, we woke to a rising sun, and I realized that Hooch had slept through the night. It was a huge milestone.

Once free from his abusers, Hooch loved life and all its offerings. He relished every day, moment, hug, and cookie as if it were his last. He was mesmerized and bewildered by the birds that flew overhead, children's laughter, and snowflakes. We spent countless hours walking, exploring nature, and simply relaxing together.

We lived next to a ballfield, and I walked Hooch there twice a day. Once there, his Bloodhound tracking instincts took over. He would put his nose to the ground and sniff—back and forth, back and forth, under brush and into the woods. He always came back with a trophy, some kind of ball. He found lacrosse balls, tennis balls, baseballs, softballs, Nerf balls, and more. Tennis balls were his favorite. He took them all home and had a collection of hundreds. At first, Hooch didn't know what a ball was. I would roll one to him, and he would just stare at it, bewildered. I kept them around the house. One day, he brushed by a ball, and it rolled. It piqued his interest, and from that day forward, he loved balls.

It was while I was trying to help Hooch that I learned the true meaning of "living in the moment." He was able to move away from his weathered past with zeal. He taught me how to move forward from life's challenges and not harbor ill will toward others.

It became clear to me that our journey was not about me rehabilitating Hooch but rather about Hooch connecting lives and educating others about the importance of human empathy toward animals. As an animal rescuer, I learned from Hooch's journey that it was less about rehabilitating my rescues and more about truly understanding the gifts they bestow upon me. Hooch was indeed a creature of divinity.

I was only given the opportunity to learn from Hooch for sixteen months. It was long enough to capture lifelong lessons about patience, understanding, humility, and vulnerability but not long enough for a lifetime of hugs, kisses, and I love yous.

I celebrate Hooch's life every day by educating others about his journey and by encouraging lawmakers to strengthen animal-welfare laws so we can put an end to the suffering of innocent creatures like Hooch. It's not right for anyone to suffer in silence, and it's not fair to tie the hands of those who want to protect the innocent from abuse.

"I wouldn't be alive"

Alyssa Denis

When I was twenty-one, I was perfectly healthy. I had moved to the city of Calgary, Canada, from a small town and was finishing my first year of studies to be a paramedic. One day, everything changed when I started coughing up blood. Doctors first thought I had been poisoned by anthrax and was a victim of terrorism. Later came a diagnosis of leukemia. There were many trips to doctors and hospitals. Two years passed before a final diagnosis was confirmed. I had severe systemic lupus (SLE).

Lupus attacks your immune system. It attacked my heart, lungs, kidneys, brain, skin cells, and nearly every major organ in my body. It focused on my heart and lungs, creating scar tissue that damaged and weakened the organs.

I started chemotherapy, the same chemo a friend of mine who suffered from leukemia was on. The goal was for the chemo to kill off the bad cells. I received chemo for three and a half years. While it helped control the lupus and inevitably saved my life, there was a negative side effect. In order to be on the chemo, I also had to be on steroids. The steroids inhibited my bones from absorbing calcium and vitamin D, and I got severe osteoporosis. My bones became thin and brittle, and I ended up breaking three vertebrae in my spine, most likely when I rolled over in bed while sleeping. Surgery didn't help. I was left with severe and chronic back pain.

I was now bound to a wheelchair and was barely able to do simple things such as putting my shirt on. With each unsuccessful treatment, and there were many of them, I became more and more depressed. I was becoming a shut-in. My only human contact was with my parents, who lived three and a half hours away, and my online friends. To make matters worse, I was told that I wouldn't live to be twenty-five years old.

It was at this time that I entered a day program, where I spent time with other people who had disabilities. One day, I met a guy who was a quadriplegic. He had a Labrador Retriever, and we struck up a conversation about his dog. He told me he had received his dog from the Lions Foundation of Canada. He suggested I apply for one, too. I couldn't think of any reason the Lions would give someone with lupus a dog. But I applied anyway.

It was a long process. There was an in-home interview, phone interviews, forms, doctor letters, and personal references. Twenty of my friends wrote to the Lions Foundation asking them to consider giving me a service dog. Nearly two years passed, and I was sure I wouldn't get a dog. That's when I heard the news. The Lions Foundation was giving me a black Labrador Retriever named Luna. But before I could bring her home, I had to attend doggie boot camp. I was flown to Oakville in Ontario, where I trained with Luna for three weeks. It was a lot of work, but it was worth it.

When you have a dog, you have to take your dog for a walk. For five years, I had been sleeping my life away and staying in bed all day. Now I had to put my clothes on, get up, and go for a walk.

Just having to get up, get out of bed, and go outside made a huge difference in my life. And with each day, Luna and I went a bit farther than the day before. Soon I was using my crutches instead of my wheelchair. Slowly and surely, having this dog with me, whom I trusted and who loved me no matter what, gave me the confidence I'd been looking for. I was moving again.

I was also making new friends. Luna was the icebreaker. People were now approaching me, asking questions about Luna, and asking to pet her. When I was alone and in a wheelchair, very few people had taken the time to say hello. With Luna, everything changed.

I had Luna for less than four months when our relationship took a dramatic turn. It was a warm August night, at midnight. I was still getting to know Luna and wasn't sure if she had to go out or not. Since we were both up and it was close to bedtime, I decided to take her for a walk—not the smartest decision I've ever made. Instead of my wheelchair, I used my crutches. I took Luna to a nearby field and let her off the leash. I had started a game of fetch with her favorite glow-in-the-dark ball when, all of a sudden, my world started spinning. Something was terribly wrong.

I collapsed and blacked out. When I came to, Luna was standing over me, licking my face, as she had been trained to do. I tried to stand but couldn't. So I put one hand on Luna's shoulder and one on her hip and asked her to steady. She stood still, but I couldn't get up. So I asked her to steady again, and this time, I put my arms around her neck. She knew, without me having to tell her, that she needed to get me home. And that's what she did. She used her strength to pull me all the way home.

Once we got to the apartment, I asked Luna to fetch the phone, and she did, without hesitation. I called my grandpa for help, and he came and took us to the hospital.

Tests revealed that I had suffered a mini-stroke. And all I could think about was how lucky I was. In the park, Luna had gone straight from play to protect mode. She could have run away or chased the rabbits that live in the park. Instead, she came to me and licked me awake. I knew Luna was awesome, but I had no idea just how amazing she was.

Because of Luna, I have my life back. She is the best thing that has ever happened to me. I'm not alone anymore, and I know I'll never be alone again. And I'm defying the odds. I'm twenty-eight now and was never meant to be this old. I am going to school to be a medical laboratory technician. And I'm using my crutches now more than my wheelchair. I know it's because Luna's here, helping me get through life. Luna is my gift from God. I wouldn't be here if it wasn't for her.

Alyssa and Luna

Lions Foundation of Canada
dogguides.com

"I had the strangest, uncontrollable urge to attend Bingo"

Dorothy Lemme

Being in a military family is extremely difficult when you are transferred overseas and are forced to leave a pet behind. This was the case for my family in 1979. My husband, David, was in the Air Force, and we were transferred to Kadena Air Base in Okinawa, Japan, for three years. We had to leave our dog, Dasher, behind with relatives in the United States.

The kids, thirteen-year-old Shari and three-year-old Scott, looked at the move as an adventure and made the transition beautifully. We all adjusted in our own ways, but there was one thing missing: our dog. So we sat down and made a family decision. We would adopt a dog from Japan.

Shortly thereafter, David came home from work one night with an eleven-month-old golden-colored mixed-breed girl he'd found at a local kennel. We named her Penny, and she seemed to understand right away that she was a member of the family. But David was quick to point out that when it came time for us to leave, we would have to leave Penny behind. David was a strong military man who ran the house. What he said was the rule of the family. It was very upsetting when he reminded us that Penny would be left. And he reminded us over and over again. I think it was his way of telling us not to get attached.

Penny had a very happy face and a fluffy tail. If her tail wasn't wagging, she placed it over her back, and we called it her umbrella. She was sweet, loving, and devoted. She had a funny way of saying "please" by doing what we called "the pose." When she wanted something, she'd sit on her back legs, lift her front legs off the ground, and drop her paws, all the while sitting up straight. We loved everything about Penny.

Shari, Penny, and Scott

Homes for the Homeless
homesforthehomeless.org

From the first night Penny was in our home, she slept beside Scott's bed as his guardian angel. Shari loved her, too, and decided to take her to a dog obedience course offered at the base. The very first day of class, the instructor told Shari not to expect too much out of her dog, as she was a mixed-breed, and most of the other dogs in the class were pure-breeds. Shari prevailed, and after twelve weeks of training, our dog Penny was the top winner of all the awards.

As we approached the end of our tour, David reminded me over and over again to start looking for a family to adopt Penny. I wanted to bring her home, but it was too expensive to fly her back to the United States. Just as I gave up hope, a miracle happened.

Eight weeks before we were scheduled to leave, I had the strangest uncontrollable urge to attend Bingo night at the Non-Commissioned Officers Club, just thirty minutes before it was supposed to start. I rarely went to Bingo, and when I did go, I went with a friend. But something was leading me that night. I had to go. I didn't even ask my friend. I just walked out the door and left David with the kids.

The very first Bingo game of the night, I won six hundred dollars. I couldn't believe it. I went home and told David about my winnings. He said I could go off-base shopping and choose something from Japan to take home with us. I looked at him and pointed to Penny. "I'm taking Penny home with us," I said. Penny was the only gift I wanted to take home from Japan.

Our next tour was at Randolph Air Force Base in San Antonio, Texas. We left without Penny because we couldn't get her on the same flight with us. She would have to travel alone. Unbeknownst to us, she sat in a warehouse in Japan for several days because of a cargo handlers strike. Then, after she reached the States, she was misrouted and ended up in Chicago. After many days and many frantic phone calls, we were granted a second miracle when we were reunited with Penny in Texas.

Penny and our other dog, Dasher, whom we had left three years earlier with relatives, got on beautifully. Penny took her place once again beside Scott's bed and was there every night until he left for college. She remained with us for seventeen years.

Penny is still in our memories every day. She changed our lives in a good way.

Her saintly attributes of patience, kindness, and forgiveness were examples of some of the important qualities I feel God wants us to emulate. I feel she was a divine messenger, sent to guide us.

When I think back to my unexplained need to go to a Bingo game, I know God gives us gifts when we least expect them. Penny was God-sent and the best six hundred dollars I've ever spent.

"I feel completely safe now"

Cheryl Elia

I was forty-five years old when I was diagnosed with multiple sclerosis. Multiple sclerosis is a chronic, progressive nervous disorder. I was no longer able to work and decided I'd love to have a dog to keep me company during the long days I was spending alone.

I went to my local animal shelter in Manahawkin, New Jersey. I walked through the shelter and stopped at the kennel of a twelve-year-old, ninety-nine-pound yellow Labrador Retriever named Lilly, who greeted me with a wagging, thumping tail. Her previous family had given her up when they made a move, choosing not to take her with them. I was told that because of her age, Lilly would be put to sleep soon. I wasn't having any of that. We walked out together.

When my MS flares, I get dizzy and have balance and vision problems. The right side of my body, from head to toe, is always numb and tingles. My whole right side feels the way it does when your foot falls asleep. This feeling never goes away, and during a flare-up, it becomes even more debilitating. It's very difficult to move.

I knew Lilly was my angel the first time we had a snow-storm. There was two feet of snow on the ground. I had to cross the street to get to my mailbox, but I couldn't use my quad cane (a cane with four feet) because the ground still had snow on it and was uneven. I was walking very slowly, and Lilly did something totally unexpected. She pressed her body against my legs and walked slowly beside me, the whole time keeping up the pressure. She prevented me from falling and helped me stay balanced. Every time I stopped, she stopped, always staying by my side until I was ready to continue. She did this all the way to the mailbox and all the way back, until I was safely in the house.

That was the first time I noticed her extraordinary ability to sense my needs. Since then, as my illness has progressed, Lilly's always by my side, helping me walk, without being taught or asked. I have fallen a few times and couldn't get up by myself. Lilly has stood beside me, braced herself, and allowed me to use her body to hold onto as I lifted myself up.

She's also there for me emotionally. It's very difficult having an illness that gets progressively worse. When I'm sad and depressed, she comforts me by putting her head on my lap, letting me know she understands and is there for me.

When I was first diagnosed with MS, I lost everything. I had to close my business. I had no money while I was waiting to be approved to receive social security. I was so depressed that I cried every day. Without Lilly's love and companionship, I don't think I would have made it this far. I feel completely safe now.

From Lilly, I have learned about true love and loyalty. It's as if she realizes that I saved her life, and now she's saving mine. She is pure love. I truly believe Lilly is a divine gift. She makes me feel loved when I feel as if no one else understands what the MS is doing to me. When others turn away and see me as a burden, Lilly stays by my side and loves me unconditionally. That's why she's my angel.

Friends of Southern Ocean County Animal Shelter

fosocas.org

Keisha and Lisa

Greater Androscoggin Humane Society
gahumane.org

"I prayed for something good to happen in my life"

Lisa Gagnon

I adopted Daisy from an SPCA in March 2003. I was told she was a Walker Coon Hound and was about four years old. She looked like a tall Beagle. I was very excited. I had two young children at home who were going to adore her. Everything was going to be great.

But when I got Daisy home, I realized she had trust issues and was especially afraid of men. At first, she wouldn't come near my husband and was pretty hesitant with me. She was so afraid that I literally had to get on my hands and knees to approach her. But I was determined to help her make the transition.

We worked together, and over time she began to trust. She was coming out of her shell when the first snowstorm of the season hit. My husband left the house to run an errand, and someone opened the door by mistake and let Daisy out. My husband saw her chasing his car, so he got out and told her to go home. She turned around and started heading toward home. He got into the car and left. But unbeknownst to him, she was following his car again.

I called for Daisy from the front door, but she wouldn't come. Forty-five minutes passed, and I was frantic. The snow was coming down hard and was piling up. That's when the phone rang. It was the local emergency veterinary clinic. Daisy was there. She had been hit by a car, and the driver had brought her in. Her back was broken. I rushed to the clinic. There were no options. My heart broke in that room. I had failed her.

I fell into a depression. I felt as if I'd lost a child. My girl had been my therapy, the Prozac I didn't have to take. Petting her ears and lying with her had been comforting and made me happy. Without her, I was despondent.

I began to pray. I asked God to please bring some joy or light my way. I'd been saying this prayer for more than a week when I was driving one brutally cold morning and saw a Beagle on the road. I pulled up to him and got out of the car. His little feet were so frozen he kept lifting them up and down. My heart leaped as I realized this dog might be the answer to my prayer. But he had tags and was soon reunited with his owners.

That night, after I'd returned him home, I realized that the thought of having a dog made me happy. And so my prayer changed. I asked God to help me get the right dog for me and my family and to give me a sign that would let me know who that dog was.

I began my search. I went to the SPCA, searched online, looked in newspapers, and eventually picked up an *Uncle Henry's*. *Uncle Henry's* is a statewide classified-advertisement publication in which people buy and sell everything from used cars to hamsters. There were hundreds of ads for pets.

I had my criteria. I didn't want a pure-bred dog. I wanted someone who needed me. One ad jumped out at me. It was a two-and-a-half-year-old, well-mannered black Labrador mix. The dog was free to a good home. She came from the neighboring town.

I called the number and told the woman I'd seen the ad. She told me someone else had already called for the dog, but she went ahead and started a conversation with me anyway. She asked me if I had any other pets, and I told her the sad story about losing Daisy. I also told her where I lived. She mentioned that she had grown up in my neighborhood, and she told me where. And that's when a light bulb went off in my head. I knew that the lady who had hit Daisy had lived in that house, and I asked the woman if she knew her. She gasped when she realized. "My mother," she said, "was the one who hit your dog." She explained that her mother was on her way to a family Christmas party that night and had been devastated by the accident. She had a blanket in the car and had rushed Daisy to the emergency vet hospital.

I fell to my knees at that moment. This was my sign. God was answering my prayer once again. This was no coincidence. This was my dog from God. I told her I wanted the dog.

She told me she'd have to call the other woman back, because, after all, she'd called first. I explained why I felt this one dog was my gift. She understood. Fifteen minutes later, she called to tell me that a Lab named Keisha was mine.

When Keisha arrived that afternoon at my home, I noticed she had badly infected nipples and was in heat. I asked if there was a chance she could be pregnant, and the woman said she didn't think so. But she had five other dogs that weren't all sterilized. It was a distinct possibility.

Keisha fit into our family immediately. She was sweet, loved attention, and always rested with her head in my lap or on my foot.

Sixty-three days after she came into our home, Keisha gave birth to nine puppies. We kept one of those puppies and named her Rosie. Keisha is now nine years old, and Rosie is six. They are everything I could ask for and more. I feel that I'm doubly blessed.

God does answer prayers, and he's always on time. It may not be when you think it's time, but it's his time. When I look into Keisha's eyes and I'm giving her my love, I'm very aware that she's my gift. She was sent from heaven. She's my God dog.

"He looked at me and handed me his paw"

Karen Talbot

It was 2009, and I was serving as president of the Parent Teachers Association at St. Joseph Elementary School in Hammonton, New Jersey. The time had come for the kids to take part in a community outreach project, and I suggested we learn about animal rescue.

The students and parents loved the idea. We called the project "Paws for a Cause" and embarked on an extraordinary mission: to rescue dogs from high-kill shelters in Georgia and transport them to loving homes in New Jersey.

Over three months, we worked with several rescue organizations in Georgia. The rescues would pull dogs from death row, pay for their veterinary care and shots, quarantine them, and then organize their transport to us. The transporters would arrive at all hours of the night and day. Families would meet the dogs, usually at a turnpike rest stop, and take them home to foster until the perfect home was found.

On one particularly rainy morning, the bus from Georgia was scheduled to arrive in Philadelphia at 3 A.M. with only one dog. I offered to do the pickup.

I met the bus driver at a hotel parking lot near the Philadelphia airport. She took a Beagle–Jack Russell mix out of a crate and handed him to me. As I looked into a bus loaded with crated dogs, I thought about what must be going through these poor dogs' minds. They were in a dark, cold, and lonely place awaiting death. The lucky ones were plucked just minutes from being led to gas chambers. They were detained in quarantine and medically stabilized for two weeks prior to making their journey. Then they were put into crates and loaded into vehicles before making a fourteen-hour trek alongside other scared animals, to an uncertain future. They had no idea of their fate. Nothing was in their control.

All of these thoughts were running through my mind as I looked down into the eyes of my new friend. A lamppost illuminated his face. His name was Buddy, and his gaze confirmed that he felt comfortable and safe with me.

Once in the car, Buddy fell into a deep sleep. Before we reached home that morning, he sat up in the passenger seat, looked at me, and handed me his paw. At that moment, I knew he was grateful.

When we got home, where Buddy would be fostered for a few days, there was a pack waiting to meet him. Since Buddy was no longer a puppy, I feared his potential interaction with my three dogs: Winnie, a yellow Labrador–Coon Hound mix; Pooh, a yellow Labrador; and Roo, a Doberman mix. They were an established pack, and I was worried they might not accept him. I cautiously introduced them. After I was sure they were going to get along, I proceeded to the kitchen to make breakfast for my son. As I was scrambling eggs, I noticed an uncomfortable silence for a house with four dogs and hardwood floors. I became fearful that the silence was not golden! I turned around and looked in the playroom. My pack of dogs had circled Buddy. He wasn't fearful. Instead, he was handing his paw to each one of my dogs. The same paw he had reassured me with he was now offering to my dogs. He was teaching us a lesson in forgiveness, healing, compassion, and trust, all with a simple gesture of giving us all he had to give, his paw.

I wasn't even contemplating the idea of keeping a fourth dog. Even if I was, I didn't think it would be fair to have Buddy miss the opportunity of having his very own home. At least, that's what I rationalized in my mind as I transported Buddy to his next temporary home with a Beagle rescue group.

The rescue was a homelike setting with thirty-five Beagles on-site. While I turned Buddy's paperwork over to the rescuer, Buddy was placed on an outside deck. I said a quick good-bye and went to my car. As I was backing out of the driveway, I glanced back at Buddy on the deck. He was looking at me and handing me his paw through the railing. My heart sank. I had a lump in my throat and was overcome with sadness as I backed out of the driveway.

I drove to work in hopes that the distraction of my daily life would compensate for my newly broken heart. One day turned into two, and I couldn't get Buddy out of my mind. Out of sight, out of mind wasn't working for me. I dismissed my thoughts by rationalizing that Buddy was in the best place to find his forever home.

A week passed, and I received a phone call that changed my life. The Beagle rescue called to tell me that Buddy wasn't getting along with one of the thirty-five Beagles living in its care. They needed someone to take him until he could be adopted. I started to shake. I dropped everything I was doing and rushed to the rescue to retrieve my little friend.

When I got there, Buddy ran to me, jumping and barking with excitement. He was overjoyed. I had loved him enough to set him free, and he came back to me.

The lessons of trust, forgiveness, healing, and compassion that have come from the rescue of one dog have been immeasurable. Buddy has taught me that if we take our cues from children and animals, the world's a much better place.

Best of all, what started as a three-month community outreach program for a school has turned into an ongoing charity to rescue dogs and other animals from high-kill shelters.

Buddy and Karen

Carpathia Paws
carpathiapaws.com

"I was the one who
was grateful"

Lorri Denton

Red came to us at the age of twelve through the Rimrock Humane Society in Roundup, Montana. We fostered him while his owner was on trial for animal cruelty.

Red, an all-red Springer Spaniel mix, was rescued from a woman who kept him in a shed with two cats in the back of her deceased father's house. She lived fifty miles away and checked on the animals every two weeks. The neighbors called police, who went to see the abandoned pets, but because there was food, water, and shelter, they could do nothing legally to help them. The neighbors continued to make calls pleading for help, as Red's pitiful barks became weakened cries. Finally, Rimrock Humane Society learned of the abuse. The organization, working with police, confiscated the animals. When they found Red, there were fifteen dead mice in the water bowl, the food was an open bag on the floor, and fresh air had come from a small hole in the shed he had poked his nose through. He had been locked away, with the cats, for two years.

My husband and I had fostered Red for six months when we received the news we had been waiting for. His owner had been convicted of animal cruelty. Red was officially our boy if we wanted him. We were relieved and overjoyed. We loved him. He was finally safe and where he belonged, with us.

Red fit into our life beautifully. He was grateful for everything. He always whined and danced with delight when we gave him food, refreshed his water, or gave him a pig's ear. He never forgot where he came from. He had horrible nightmares, and lightning terrified him. I'd get up with him, and we'd cower under a blanket together until the storm passed. And when the nightmares came, I would lie next to him and comfort him. He would look up at me with absolute gratitude and devotion. What Red didn't know was that he was a comfort to me, too. And I was the one who was grateful for him.

I was forty-six years old and weighed three hundred forty pounds. I wanted to change. I wanted to be able to fit into clothes, to fit into any booth or chair in a restaurant, to fit into an airline seat. I wanted to fit in.

I started on my journey to lose weight because I was scared of what would inevitably happen if I didn't. I had been to a workshop for my job and listened to a doctor speak about metabolic syndrome, in which a person has the combination of high blood pressure, high cholesterol, and diabetes. I didn't have diabetes yet, but I knew it was coming if I didn't do something about it.

I started by keeping a journal of everything I ate and how I was feeling. I also began an exercise routine. For one hour each day, I watched Richard Simmons on a DVD as he led me through low-impact aerobics using small weights. As I exercised, Red watched me intently from his place, either sitting or lying next to me. At the end of each session, as I did my stretches, I'd roll over toward him and was rewarded with licks and nuzzles. It was a struggle to do the exercise, but knowing that Red was waiting anxiously for the morning routine to begin and watching as I worked out kept me going.

And while Red was devoted to seeing me through my exercise routine, he took his own exercise alone.

My husband and I owned a boarding kennel, located on a hill two hundred yards beyond our house. Each morning, we watched Red take his solitary walk. He'd start at the front porch, take a long stretch, and then walk over our mowed lawn and into the tall weeds along the fence line. He'd then walk five hundred feet up the hill

Red

Rimrock Humane Society
rimrockhumanesociety.org

and around the building, eventually appearing at the front row of the outdoor kennels. We watched as he sniffed each kennel, saying good morning to each dog. The dogs would often bark at him, then settle down as he moved to the next dog. I can only guess he was comforting the dogs.

Two years passed, and our routines didn't change. Red took his solitary, comforting walks and then joined me as I exercised. It was a struggle to do the exercise tapes, but knowing Red was there for me, waiting and watching, I couldn't skip a day. He never left my side.

I was forty-five and Red was twelve when he came to us. He was sixteen when he left us. He taught me to live each day with a hopeful and grateful heart. And he helped save my life. In our time together, I lost one hundred fifty pounds.

I've never gone a day without remembering Red's eyes, looking lovingly at me as I struggled to exercise. I learned a valuable lesson from that wonderful dog. If he could love me after all he'd been through, I could love me.

"I saw his soul come alive"

Deana Whitfield

I work for a national nonprofit organization that's dedicated to freeing chained, penned, and neglected backyard dogs. Dogs Deserve Better works for the release of chained dogs and then coordinates with foster and rescue groups to get those dogs loving homes.

I volunteer for the organization, educating owners and doing rescues in San Bernardino and Riverside Counties in California. In California, we have a tethering law by which it's illegal to chain or tie your dog up for more than three hours in a twenty-four-hour period. It's also illegal not to provide shelter for your dog. If you don't provide food and water for your dog, you're also breaking the law. When I approach owners, I explain the laws and talk to them about the psychological cruelty behind chaining the dog alone without other dogs or human companionship.

I have rescued many dogs from the chain, and every one of them has been grateful to me. They have all become different dogs once they were freed. This story is about one guy who left an unforgettable impression on me after I watched his soul come alive in a period of seconds.

In July 2010, I received a call from a good Samaritan named Vivianna who was worried about a twelve-month-old Pit Bull Terrier named Capone. She told me he had no food or water and that her family often fed him. She reported that the dog was chained in a concrete yard with no shelter from the sun and had been on that slab since he was a puppy. She said she had watched, day in and day out, as his owner ignored him.

It was a searing 104 degrees outside when I reached the tan-and-cream-colored dog named Capone. He had no food. There was no water. And, not surprisingly, the dog was an empty shell. He looked at me with absolutely no expression on his face. He had no energy. He didn't want to play. And why would he? The pads on his feet were burned. He was defeated and broken. You could see he had nothing to live for. He had surrendered to his confinement. It may sound crazy, but when he looked into my eyes with such despair, it was as if he was begging me to help him. I truly believe our souls connected and I knew exactly what he was asking me to do. For that brief moment, that divine moment between us, he wagged his tail.

I turned back and looked at Capone as I was leaving. His head was hung low, and he was staring at me, asking me why I hadn't done what he had asked. I promised him I'd be back.

I went to the house to speak to the owner, who was breaking at least three California animal-cruelty laws. Vivianna came with me, offering to translate my English to Spanish. I explained to the owner that the state of California had a tethering law. It was against the law for him to chain the dog outside. I gave him a copy of the law. I also explained the other violations and why it was considered cruel to deny an animal food, water, and shelter.

After I made my case for Capone, I asked the owner if he would release him to me. I explained that if he would release him, I would need a few days to find him a foster home. My request was met with arrogant dismissal. He didn't care about the dog, anyway. Sure, I could have the dog, but if I didn't take him on the spot, he would cut him loose into the neighborhood.

The area where Capone was confined was known for its illegal dog-fighting rings. If he was released and became a stray, there was a good chance he could be picked up and used as a bait dog. This couldn't happen.

Capone

Dogs Deserve Better
dogsdeservebetter.org

I came to an agreement with the owner. He would give me three days to find a foster home for him. After that, he was cutting him loose.

It's not easy to find a foster home for a Pit Bull, especially on short notice. The public's perception of them, thanks to the people who abuse them and train them to fight, makes them fearful of the breed.

I scrambled to find a foster home by making phone calls to volunteers and by sending out mass e-mails. I also visited Capone to make sure he had food and water. I wanted the owner to know I wasn't going away and that I'd make good on my word to pick Capone up on the third day. Each day, Capone sat there defeated. And each day, I promised him I'd be back. The look in his eyes haunted me. I couldn't sleep at night.

On day three, my time was up, and I was ready. My niece and a volunteer came with me. As I approached Capone, he didn't smile or wag his tail. He remained empty and hollow, void of spirit. I gently placed a new collar around his neck, attached a leash, and gave a little tug. He was confused. He sat down near his chain and looked at me. I told him this wasn't his life any longer. After a few more tugs and a coax with a jerky treat, Capone slowly walked out of his concrete prison. And then I witnessed nothing short of a miracle. As Capone's feet touched the grass, he lifted his head high, inhaled the freshness, and looked up at me, asking, "Am I really free?" In his eyes, there was nothing but pure happiness and joy. He was vibrant, alive, happy, and energetic in an instant. I saw his soul awaken.

Capone was placed in a wonderful foster home and taken to a veterinarian, where he was neutered, given shots, and treated for a bad case of roundworms.

On October 8, 2010, Capone was adopted to his forever home. He lives indoors with a loving and caring family. He is spoiled rotten and is free to roam the house and an acre of land. I visit as often as I can, and when I do, he sits with me, stares gratefully into my eyes, and gives me big, wet kisses.

I have always been passionate about freeing chained dogs, but Capone's story and his gratefulness to me have always been a bit unbelievable. I saw deep into his lonely soul, and many times over, he has thanked me for freeing him. Dogs do have many of the same feelings we do. They feel despair, heartache, sadness, and loneliness. They also feel gratitude.

Loyalty

*Dependability with
Kindness*

Cous Cous

Just as the athlete has his coach, the Hindu his yogi, and the student his mentor, there are many of us who find wisdom in dogs. Because of their teachings, we are better people.

The most enlightening guru I've ever known is a tiny, white, fluffy Maltese-Pomeranian named CousCous. Cous was an unexpected and unwanted gift. As it turned out, she's the best gift I've ever received. She's taught me that master teachers come in all forms.

When I was thirty-four, I found myself single for the first time in my adult life. I'd met a gorgeous Australian man a year before, while working for CNN in Casablanca, Morocco, and I was enamored. But I'm a realist. I knew it wouldn't work. So, for the first time in my life, I decided just to have fun. I was invited to Australia and decided to go.

The real men in my life, my dogs Philophal and Nick, went to their dad's house while I hopped five planes and traveled to the other side of the world.

It was Christmas Day, 1996. I had been in Perth, Australia, for a week and was having a great time when . . . "Merry Christmas," Jon announced, presenting a tiny ball of white fluff from behind his back. My heart sank as I took the puppy with a red ribbon around her body into my hand. The puppy's black eyes looked up at me adoringly, and I instantly loved her and resented him.

He knew I had two dogs in the United States that I'd never leave. He knew how devoted to them I was. Still, he gave me a dog.

I stroked the tiny head of the little girl, who resembled a newly hatched baby bird. "What were you thinking?" I asked. Jon's smile faded. He looked at me innocently. But he was no innocent—he was a psychiatrist! It was a brilliant maneuver to sweeten the Australian package. It was calculated and manipulative, and it worked.

I was smitten. But because of strict quarantine regulations in Australia, I couldn't bring Cous back with me. She'd have to stay behind with Jon, and I'd have to go back to Philophal and Nick, not knowing for sure if I'd ever return.

Every five months for the next four years, I hopped five planes and traveled forty-six hours to reach the other side of the world. Once I was in Australia, Cous refused to leave my side. She slept with her body against my foot, always touching. Every morning, as the birds began to sing and the sun rose, she would gingerly walk up the bed until she was standing on my chest, hovering above my head, with a joyful smile on her face. It was her game. The moment I opened my eyes, she lowered her front paws and cheerfully showered me with a bouquet of very deliberate, loving kisses. She was religious about this ritual, and I loved it. Jon, on the other hand, saw it as an obsessive habit that needed to be broken. Veterinarians and Dog Whisperers were consulted to see why Cous licked. There was no answer. She was just happy.

And she was thankful. Every single time I fed her, whether it was a meal or a treat, when she finished, she'd find me and gently lick my leg. She was joyful and grateful and happy, and I loved having her in my life.

But there was something more. Cous was a divine soul, and when she looked at me, I felt love, an all-encompassing, universal love that made me believe in me. She wasn't just a faithful friend, she was the closest thing to heaven I allowed myself to know. Through her, I received joy in my heart and began to love others. At the same time this was happening, I had an epiphany: if this dog could love and accept me despite all my flaws, then I could try to accept myself. From that point onward, I decided that Cous would be my barometer. If I woke up and she loved me, then her mood would dictate my day. The clouds that had hung over my head parted, and I found peace and joy in every day.

While Cous was devoted to Jon while I was away, he said her loyalty was ultimately with me. He may have fed, walked, and trained her for months, but the moment I arrived, she refused to leave my side. But my loyalty was not with her. It couldn't be. I don't know how, but somehow she knew this and accepted it. As I inevitably prepared to leave, Cous would sit in my suitcase for days, begging me to take her with me. It broke my heart. I was living a divided life.

When I was away, I made every attempt to make sure she knew I'd be back. I left my clothes tucked in her bed. I'd speak to her on the phone, and she'd respond by aggressively licking the receiver. The truth is, she kept me coming back because she was deliciously wonderful and we were devoted to each other. The Australian man was a bonus with a great accent.

Philophal passed away, and then Nick. I moved to Australia.

Australians and Americans may speak the same language, but culturally we're very different, and I found the transition to another country difficult. I was still doing some work for CNN, but everything about life seemed harder. I didn't have any friends or family, I had to drive on the opposite side of the road, and e-mail hadn't come into play. To talk to someone I loved cost about fifty bucks. It wasn't easy. I was now in a land as far away as I could be from my country, my family, and my friends. But there was Cous, my best friend and most loyal companion. We explored the country together, taking in a new park or beach every day.

Ten years after Cous was born, Jon and I made her legitimate by getting married. And with the addition of a nearly blind, one-eyed Shih Tzu who became the child I couldn't conceive, the four of us became a modern dog family.

Cous is fifteen and a half now. She can barely walk. She is fading away and will be leaving me soon. Still, every morning, she crawls her way up to my face and gently licks me lovingly. I'd have missed out on a lot of sunrises if it hadn't been for my sunshine.

Cous is my happiness guru. She has taught me how to live in the moment, how to be happy, and how to have fun. The most important lessons my fluffy divine gift has taught me are meant for sharing:

1. It's logical to start each day with a kiss and a smile on your face.
2. Be grateful for everything.
3. Always let others know you're thankful for their kindness to you.
4. Loyalty is based on having faith and trust in each other. It's a two-way street. The formula works for all species.

"Giving up on him would be giving up on myself"

Saskia Noomen

I was on a safari in South Africa on a pitch-black night, looking for animals on a private reserve. That's what I was doing when I learned my beloved fourteen-year-old dog was lost in a city with danger on every street corner, in France.

My whole life, I'd wanted a dog. So at twenty-five, my birthday present to myself was Silas, a Terrier cross bigger than a Jack Russell yet smaller than a Collie, with a foxlike face, wiry reddish hair, a long thick tail, and skinny legs.

I was living in Australia when I found Silas at a dog refuge. I had actually dreamed of having a German Shepherd, an Irish Wolfhound, or even a Saint Bernard. But I was renting a house, and the owners would only allow me to have a small dog. At the refuge, there were at least fifty dogs, jumping and clawing at the iron bars of their concrete homes. The only small dog that remained there was named Stubby. *Stubby* is the slang word for a can of beer in Australia. While every dog in the refuge begged for me to take him, Stubby cowered in a corner, uninterested in human contact, aggressive if you came near him. He was half-price and listed for lethal injection. The staff told me someone had dumped him in front of their gates.

I took him and renamed him Silas (dweller of the forest) because there was something wild about him. I picked him up a week later, after he'd been castrated. He was skinny and shivering from fear. The first week we were together, he was manic. He paced the living room all day long. He was scared of everyone, including me. I didn't let his fear stop me. I began training him, and within a week, he knew how to sit, stay, come, heel, everything. He learned quickly.

I love to ride horses. From the first day I took Silas to my horse, Monty, he understood. Monty and I galloped, and Silas ran happily alongside, sometimes sprinting out in front, running through the forest and then darting back out to join us. He quickly became my best friend, and I began to see Silas as a mirror image of myself. He wasn't an easy-to-love creature. He was cool and independent, but he was a true friend.

We moved from Australia to Paris. Silas was with me always, except when it was really impossible. And one of those rare times was when I decided to go to South Africa for two weeks.

Six days into my holiday, when I called to check on my man, the sitter told me she'd lost him. She'd taken him off the leash, and he'd run away.

It took me two days and two planes to get back to Paris. I drove straight to Antony, a town thirty kilometers south of Paris, where Silas had been lost. I was distraught. Silas was now fourteen, had very bad eyesight, and was nearly deaf. How would he survive?

I was told someone had seen him eating rubbish in a village

a kilometer from where he'd been lost. I immediately drove to Verrières-le-Buisson and started putting up posters there. As I was doing this, I saw him! He was so terrified he ran past me. I hadn't expected this. He couldn't see or hear me. I chased him. Some teenage boys joined the chase on bicycles. One caught him, but Silas bit him and took off. The boys called later to say they'd watched him cross a big road and enter a park. I went there. Nothing. Little did I know that I wouldn't see Silas again for ten days.

I booked a room at a local hotel and contacted veterinarians, the mayor, the police, and the animal refuge, to let them know of my search. Several people told me they'd seen Silas but couldn't catch him. I called my own veterinarian and a dog-behavior specialist and asked where they thought he might go. They said the same thing. He would go back to the location where he'd found food. So I went back to the shopping center's rubbish deposit, where Silas was first seen, and I waited. But he never showed up.

I then printed one thousand posters and drove around, putting them up everywhere. After a few days passed, I received a call from a kind man who was the president of the local rescue organization for lost dogs. He joined in the search. That day, someone called and said they'd seen Silas. They gave me an address, not far from the shopping center. All day and late into the night, we searched.

The next day, I received a phone call from a restaurant owner who lived in a village called Juvisy-sur-Orge. This was fifteen kilometers from Verrières-le-Buisson. He said he'd seen Silas cross the road in front of his restaurant. I drove there immediately. The highway was an autoroute, with four lanes on each side. I had a hard time believing that my half-blind and almost deaf dog could cross it safely, let alone run fifteen kilometers in seven days. Still, I looked for him. After an hour, I received a call from a man who said he was trying to catch Silas at a park in the same town. I begged him not to give chase but instead to give me the address. And then I lost the mobile-phone connection. He never called back.

I was skeptical about the restaurant owner and the subsequent phone call. So I called my vet and asked if he thought it was possible for Silas to run fifteen kilometers in seven days. He said no, that he was too old and incapacitated. So I went back to Verriere Buisson and spent another night looking for him there. By now, he'd been missing for ten days. It was raining, and it was cold.

Saskia and Silas

Chien Perdu (Lost Dog)
chien-perdu.org

At six that night, I received a phone call from a young man asking me if I was looking for my dog. He said he'd seen him get hit by a car in front of the shopping center. I asked if he was alive, but the boy said he didn't know. I raced there and was greeted by a group of youths. They laughed as I got out of my car. No Silas. It was a cruel joke.

I then received a call from an animal control officer in Juvisy-sur-Orge, where the restaurant was. "Do you own a dog named Silas?" the man asked. I hesitated, thinking it was another joke. "I have your dog."

When I arrived at the address the man gave me, Silas was in a cage in his van. He howled and cried when he recognized me. I pulled him out of the cage, put a leash on him, held him close to my heart, and burst into tears. My whole outlook in life had changed in those ten days. Other problems seemed trivial. As I held him in my arms, I knew I'd never have a reason to be truly unhappy again, because a miracle had happened to me.

Silas's journey had been a long one. In the end, he had crossed the superhighway and had probably been hit by a car. He had lost all of his upper teeth on the left side. He had, in fact, been chased by the man who had called me from Juvisy-sur-Orge, who was trying to help. The man didn't catch him. But Silas, while being chased, fell into a walled-in garden. A lady who lived in the apartment adjacent to the garden found him the next day. She gave him a blanket and fed him some fish. He slept another night in the garden. And the next day, she called for help.

People have asked me why I never gave up searching for my dog. It's because Silas is an extension of myself. Giving up on him would be giving up on myself and everything I believe in. Loyalty and love, whether between people or with animals, are the most important things in life to me.

I feel my path didn't cross Silas's by accident. He's seen me through many difficult times in my life. Silas has given me a reason to get up and go out when I was feeling down. He was my family when I lived alone overseas, far from my own family. He has seen me through relationships and the loss of my father. He, who has been abused to the extent that he is still afraid when I reach out to pat his head, gives me unconditional love and trust. Other dog owners are possibly the only people who will understand when I say that my little dog has been the most important person in my life for the past sixteen years.

Silas is now blind, deaf, and arthritic, and he remains the love of my life.

"I could not chase his love away"

Shannon Martin

After being an extremely active and fit young mother of two busy boys, I was told it would only be a couple of years before I wouldn't be able to walk. I was forty-one years old and was diagnosed with severe rheumatoid arthritis. I had what is called lower back and cervical stenosis. Effectively, the discs in my back were disintegrating.

Being told you're going to lose your ability to walk is one thing; dealing with it is another matter altogether. I ignored the diagnosis for as long as I could—until it became a reality. As my health spiraled downward, my sense of well-being went with it.

My sons married and moved into their own homes, and I no longer felt "needed" or "necessary." I could no longer keep up with the demands of working as a teacher's assistant for a kindergarten class or my job as a lay chaplain in several hospitals. Now that I was in a wheelchair, I didn't feel I could meet my responsibilities. The depression became so deep I didn't think I could survive. My father had committed suicide, and I honestly considered it an option. You see, I was not only depressed but also in a great deal of pain. I was also alone during the day with no one to help me.

That's when a friend of mine who had a service dog told me I needed one. I researched service dogs to find out what they could do for me, and I was pleasantly surprised. So I applied for a dog through Texas Hearing and Service Dogs (THSD).

Two months later, I was accepted into the program, and a little more than a year later, I was informed that a yellow Labrador named Noble, with really red hair, would be my partner.

Noble and Shannon

Texas Hearing and Service Dogs
servicedogs.org

I'd had dogs as a child, but they'd always lived outside. Now, I was told, an animal would live inside with me. The concept was new to me, and I'd have to adjust.

The first thing that changed in my life was that I had to get up and get moving every day to train with the dog. I didn't always want to get up but thought, "Well, I owe the animal and the THSD people this much." So each day, I got up. Then, slowly, over a period of months, I began to see that this dog—a dog, mind you—was in love with me. He was in love with depressed and worthless me. I would shoo him away, and he would look at me from across the room with eyes that said, "I love you and want to be beside you."

Noble taught me that I couldn't chase his love away. His love for me renewed over and over again. Each sin, each time I turned him away, was forgiven in love—because he chose to love me.

It was then that I realized that God loved me—worthless me. I also learned that the words *service* and *love* are synonymous.

Since Noble showed me the value of my life, I've taken the word *worthless* out of my vocabulary. And while I had worked as a chaplain, I'd never totally understood the lesson: God loves me for me, and even when I sin, he'll never turn away. He served me by sending love into my life, and I am to serve him by showing the same love to all his children. I've got it now!

"They broke the door down"

Maureen Duncum

It was 1970, and I found myself living in a prison community in Ontario, Canada, with my young family. The town of Burwash was built by inmates to house the people who worked at the Burwash Industrial Farm. My husband was farm staff and oversaw the inmates in the fields as they worked the crops. Those crops, along with bread made at the prison, sustained the community.

I lived in a row house (two houses in a row that shared the same entrance) with my husband, four wee children, and a black Standard Poodle named Princess. Two of the children, Clayton (seven) and Clinton (four), were my own. The other two were fosters. I took in children because I loved them, and at the time, good homes were badly needed. Diann was a sweet three-year old girl who wasn't wanted by her parents. Four-year-old Darrin had Down syndrome. He'd been kept in a closet before he came to us and was afraid of everything.

Princess loved the children, especially Darrin. She was very loving and always pleasing. Aside from chasing her ball, her favorite thing to do was to watch over and play with the children.

If anyone needed my attention, Princess had a way of letting me know. She would come to me, give me a stare, then take a few steps back toward the children, turn around quickly, and stare again. I could always count on her. She deeply cared for them, and they all loved her.

Early one morning at two o'clock, Princess came to my bed and woke me by nudging me with her nose and giving me her stare. I automatically assumed she wanted to go out. But when I opened the door to the outside, she ran down the steps and then came right back up the stairs and went to the neighbor's door, where she started scratching at it frantically. I went to get her, and that's when I smelled smoke coming from the neighbor's house.

My knocking turned to banging and then pounding. No one came to the door. I ran into my house and called security. Within minutes, the guards were there, and they broke the door down with an axe. Our neighbor was unconscious, overcome by smoke. He'd left something on the stove, and the smoke had filled the house. He was taken away by ambulance. Thanks to Princess, my family and my neighbor were all okay.

We had Princess for six years before we moved to England, and I had to give her back to the breeder from where she had come. Forty years have passed, and I've never had a dog since, because saying good-bye to Princess was one of the most heartbreaking things I've ever had to do.

Princess was our miracle dog. She did wonders for all of us. I'll never forget, as long as I live, how much she loved and pro-tected us.

Mostly Mutts
mostlymutts.org

"I stood there shocked"

Amanda Fadden

It was a cold and icy morning in Delran, New Jersey, not the kind of weather I'd become used to in Florida. It was Christmastime, and my grandmother, my guide dog, Hughes, and I had traveled north to spend the holiday with my uncle. I could hear the ice cracking on the ground outside while Hughes lay happily sprawled on the floor snoring.

I had only had Hughes, a black Labrador Retriever, for three months. He was my first dog. I was eighteen, and he was two years old. We were at the getting-to-know-you stage. One thing I had learned was that first thing in the morning, he needed to eat and then go for a walk.

Hughes had just had breakfast. It was now time for a walk. Having discovered that he hated getting his paws wet, I took a moment to put on booties to protect his feet from the cold ground. He disliked the booties almost as much as the wet ground. It took a while, but I eventually got the boots on and harnessed him up.

As we walked out of the house, I yelled out to my grandma that we were going for a walk. As I closed the door, I heard her say, "Okay, be careful."

Because of a genetic eye condition called retinitis pigmentosa, I'm legally blind but nevertheless do have the ability to see some things. For instance, in a store, I can see the different colors on boxes but can't tell the difference between them without feeling them or asking someone what's in the box. The only food that I can tell apart from others is Reese's Peanut Butter Cups, because the packaging is a unique orange and I know they're kept in the candy aisle at the store.

I had been to my uncle's house before but had never been for a walk. I didn't know my way around but felt pretty confident with Hughes by my side. We started down the slippery driveway, and before long, we had walked up and down streets, across streets, and around blocks. All of a sudden, I realized what I'd done. Not only had I lost track of time, but I'd walked out of my area. I was lost.

Frustrated with myself for not paying attention, I stood for a long time, looking down at Hughes, then down the street, then back to Hughes. "I'll have to trust you, Mister," I told him. And even though I said it, I didn't really feel it. Hughes listened, took a right, and started walking down a street. I followed, still boiling in my own water. Then he stopped. I looked to my left. I could make out a house and cars that might be familiar but thought my sight was screwy. I asked Hughes to move ahead, but he wouldn't budge. So I decided to walk up to the house and ask if the people there might know where my uncle lived.

I turned toward the house. "Hughes, forward," I instructed. Hughes happily walked forward, picking up his pace. He was so excited his tail was wagging. I rang the doorbell. A woman opened the door and said, "Amanda, it's about time you got home." I dropped the leash, and Hughes ran inside while I stood there in shock. A wave of joy and happiness washed over me as I realized he'd brought me home.

I went to Hughes and grabbed him, kissed him, hugged him, and gave him loads of loving. "What a good boy," I repeated over and over. I gave him some treats, and he went wild playing with them. At that moment, I realized that this dog knew much more than I was willing to give him credit for. The door to my mind and heart had been thrown open. I now trusted Hughes with all my body and soul and knew his loyalty would keep me safe and always get me home.

Guide Dogs for the Blind
guidedogs.com

"She completes me"

Jennifer Warsing

It was a cold winter morning as I bundled up to take my first hearing guide dog, a chocolate Labrador named Hattie, outside for a walk. As I glanced out the window, I could see the freshly laid snow being blown across the street and sidewalks. I thought it was symbolic of how bitter and cold the world can be.

Hattie had only been with me for a few months. I was thirty, and she was one. As we walked outside, I could feel the crunch of snow beneath my boots, and it sent shivers through my body. I glanced at Hattie and noticed she was smiling. Her tail was held high and was wagging. It dawned on me that nothing in the world could dampen her spirits or keep her from living in the moment. She held sheer innocence, pure love, and devotion in her heart. As I witnessed this, I looked down and noticed our footprints, side-by-side, in the snow. It was then I realized that no matter how lonely or cold the world could seem, I'd never walk alone again. Hattie would always be there by my side. I was overcome by a sense of peace. The next thing I knew, I, too, had a smile on my face and was feeling the pure joy of the moment we were sharing together. Little did I know, this dog was going to be my greatest blessing.

I received Hattie from Dogs for the Deaf, an organization that rescues dogs from animal shelters and then trains them to assist people who are hard of hearing or deaf. I wasn't born deaf. I lost my hearing as a result of Ménière's disease, a disorder of the inner ear that causes balance issues and deafness. I literally went to bed at the age of five a hearing child and woke the next morning a deaf child.

Before Hattie came into my life, I used assistive signaling devices that would blink for numerous sounds in my home such as the doorbell, the telephone, and the smoke detector. I found these devices to be less than satisfactory because if I wasn't in the room at the time the device was flashing, I had no idea I was being alerted to a sound. They were also electrical and affected by power outages. Even with assistive devices, I missed telephone calls and visitors at my door and had many sleepless nights worrying that the smoke detector would go off and I wouldn't know it.

I lived in fear, constantly on edge, wondering what sounds I might be missing. The silence led to loneliness and solitude. I wasn't comfortable in my home, in my skin, or in the world around me. During the day, if a repairman was scheduled to come between nine AM and three PM, I would sit at the front door and wait for him the whole time, afraid of missing the knock or the doorbell. I felt imprisoned in my small world of silence. I was in a constant battle to function as a hearing person in a world that, for me, didn't have sound.

But then Hattie arrived, and my life blossomed. Hattie's trained to alert me to the oven timer, the microwave, the doorbell, a door knock, the telephone, the alarm clock, the smoke detector, and someone calling my name. She takes her job as my "four-legged ears" quite seriously.

Hattie has opened doors to new experiences for me. One of my favorite examples is the first time I had food delivered to my home.

When Hattie told me the deliveryman was at the front door, I was brought to tears. That evening, I ate the most delicious pizza and realized that my life would now be filled with simple blessings and new experiences.

Everything changed on that cold and blustery morning when Hattie taught me I could live in the moment. I went from being pessimistic and worried all the time to having days filled with open and never-ending possibilities. Hattie transformed my life from one of silence and solitude to one filled with sound and joy. She is divine because she completes me.

I have yet to figure out who saved whom. Was Hattie's life spared by being rescued from a shelter and trained to be a hearing dog, or was I spared from a life of dread and silence by an unlikely angel who just happens to have four legs, a wet nose, a tail, and a heart of gold?

Hattie

Dogs for the Deaf
dogsforthedeaf.org

Passing

The Wisdom of
Knowing

Bunny Man and Jennifer

One of my favorite quotes is from humorist Will Rogers, who said, "If there are no dogs in heaven, then when I die, I want to go where they went." I agree. The truth is, the hardest part of life is losing someone you love and who loved you.

We have faith that there's more to come after death, we hope there's more, yet our logic questions everything we want to believe. Two contributors from my last book, *God Stories*, have enlightened me. Both had near-death experiences, where they say they had a glimpse of heaven. Both have told me there were dogs and other animals there. That's almost good enough for me. But I still crave my own personal proof. I don't think I'll get it until I'm gone. But I have received hopeful signs.

It was a beautiful October morning when I knew, after several sleepless nights and many visits to the vet, that the time had come. My loyal companion of the past twelve years, a Terrier-Poodle named Philophal, whom I lovingly called Bunny Man, was in his final hours after struggling with Cushing's disease for two years. His immune system was shot. Antibiotics weren't working anymore, and he could barely breathe. He was struggling. Today was the day.

I packed a jumbo bag of his favorite treat, Pup-a-roni, and placed him in the front passenger seat of my car while his buddy Nick sat in the back. As I drove for an hour to the vet, I kept handing Bunny Pup-a-ronis. The disease made him feel as if he was starving. He could barely breathe, but he hadn't lost his appetite.

I'd first seen Bunny Man on my morning drive to work at a radio station in Ogden, Utah. I was twenty-two years old, and he was about one. He was sitting in the road facing a group of people who were sitting on a bus-stop bench. The sight broke my heart. He was clearly asking for help. At that moment I told myself, "If he's still around when I come home from work, I'll help him." I'd already rescued two dogs that year, taking them into my home. I didn't have room for another.

On my way home, I glanced down the side streets and took a good look as I passed the bus stop. I didn't see him. As I pulled into my driveway, there he was, sitting patiently. It was meant to be.

I took him to the vet and asked why he had so many bumps just below the surface of his skin. An X-ray confirmed that he was riddled with buckshot. Someone had shot him. That was it. No one would ever hurt him again.

It took me two days to shear the matted hair from his skin. He was so matted there weren't any openings in his hair for him to urinate or defecate. The stench was nearly unbearable as I carefully cut the hair away. Once finished, I gave him a bath, and from that moment, he was my most loyal companion. He was forever grateful.

Faithful, devoted, and adoring, Bunny became my fierce protector. It was as if he had been assigned to me, to stand guard at my personal door. Bunny saw me through several relationships in my twenties, along with a painful and debilitating marriage. And now, twelve years later, I knew this would be one of the hardest days of my life. I wasn't sure I could go on without him.

We lay down together on the floor of an examination room,

and I nuzzled my head into his curly fur. He struggled to breathe. I struggled to breathe. The room was dimly lit from a very small, basement-like window above. The vet came in quietly, euthanized my darling man, and left us alone. Tears poured from my eyes as my heart broke. A few moments passed, and when I opened my eyes, what I saw made me feel immersed in love. The room was dark, with the exception of a ray of light that was coming through the window, illuminating Bunny's head. I watched as particles of light twinkled inside the beam and knew I was witnessing something miraculous. It was the first of several signs I'd get that day.

After Nick had a chance to see that Bunny had passed, we started off for the long, lonely journey home. A half hour into the trip, I pulled into a McDonald's drive-thru, one of Nick's favorite places, to get a couple of hamburgers for him before we continued on. A short time later, I was crying uncontrollably and couldn't catch my breath. I thought of pulling over when I noticed the license plate on the car in front of me. The letters spelled BUNNIES. I couldn't believe what I was seeing. Of all the license plates, how many would have those letters spelled out that way?

Before reaching home, I took Nick for a well-deserved walk around the water's edge of Eagle Lake. It was a perfect fall day, warm and partly cloudy. Most of the leaves were on the ground, scattering color everywhere. Nick ventured off into a pile of leaves and lifted his leg. All of a sudden, I saw the leaves move as if someone were walking in them. The movement startled Nick, who ran to me with his tail between his legs. I knelt down and stroked his head, and together we stared at the same spot for what seemed like forever. There was comfort in knowing that Bunny was still with us.

On the way home, a rabbit ran into the road and turned toward the car. I stopped, mesmerized. It didn't move for the longest time; it just stared at me. I'd never seen a real bunny on the island where I lived. It was a sign, another gentle message.

Maybe all the signs I received that day were just coincidences enhanced by a vivid imagination. But I don't think so.

"My heart stopped hurting, but it was broken nonetheless"

Carol McCafferty

D akota was a wonderful and vital part of my life. He was a grayish-black mix of Sheep Dog and Afghan Hound who looked like an Irish Wolfhound with floppy ears. He was my handsome fella. Dakota's favorite thing to do was to swim in the Soda Butte Creek in Silver Gate, Montana, where we lived. And he loved watching the buffalo herds in nearby Yellowstone National Park.

At the age of seventeen and a half, it became apparent that I had to make the decision to take his life. That was how I looked at it. I was going to kill my dog, try to pick up the pieces, and move on with my life without him. Yeah, sure.

I dragged my heels on making the decision for six months and prayed on it every day. I prayed for guidance. And so the day came.

It was a beautiful fall day as my husband, Mac, and I prepared to drive the three hours to the veterinarian. But I couldn't see the beauty of the day. As Mac drove, I was being ripped inside out. I didn't want to go. I just wanted to stop the truck, grab my dog, and run into the mountains. And yet I felt guilty, because I was thinking about myself, not Dakota. All kinds of thoughts raced through my mind. Should I let him die on his own, or should I assume the right to take his life? After all, he was still happy. He was just incontinent and could barely stand. But was he suffering?

I didn't think the ride would ever end. In my heart, I didn't ever want it to end. We could just stay in the truck and never stop driving. That would work. And then, all of a sudden, we were there.

I was numb. Tears flowed uncontrollably. Mac carried Dakota inside and put him on the table. I felt as if I was being put down. I kissed him all over his face, and he kissed me back over and over again, as if he knew he wasn't going to see me for a while and he wanted me to know how much he loved me. We spent twenty minutes this way, just he and I.

When the doctor came in, I thought I was going to die. My heart actually hurt. I was in physical pain. Dakota looked into my eyes and licked my hand. I kept telling him I loved him, and he let out a little cry. He was crying with me.

I then held my head to his chest and hugged him tightly as the vet gave the injection. I felt and heard his heart slowly stop. Instantly, my heart stopped hurting, but it was broken nonetheless.

As we were walking out of the vet's office into a large gravel parking lot, I numbly bent down and picked something up. I don't remember the ride from there to Bozeman. As we sat down at a table to have lunch, Mac tried to console me and reached across the table for my hands. I withdrew my right hand. Mac asked what I had in my hand. It was then I realized I was holding something in my clenched fist.

I opened my hand to find a miracle. It was a stone shaped like a heart. The shape wasn't flat. It was three-dimensional. One side of the stone had a broken white line down its center, and the other side of the stone had all the arteries of a human heart. At that moment, I knew God was speaking to me. He was letting me know that I didn't take Dakota's life. I did do the right thing. Dakota was in good hands and loved me still, with all his heart.

A few days later, I called the vet's office and asked them if the heart-shaped rock was something they did for all clients. The staff swore to me they had nothing to do with it. I guess I called them because I wanted proof that the heart-shaped stone was indeed divine intervention.

I know that I'll see Dakota and the other animals again. I can hardly wait. Dakota is still with me 24/7 because I always carry my heart-shaped stone with me.

Dogs Trust
dogstrust.org.uk

"I was very troubled"

Shirley Parr

Nowa, my son Steven's five-year-old Shepherd-Lab mix, was not allowed in my mother's room. This was a rule he understood and obeyed.

My mother was not a dog person. She thought that dogs, especially large ones, belonged outside. Despite this, Nowa won her over, as he did everyone. She often told family and friends that he was good company to her while I was at work.

When Nowa was five years old, my mother was diagnosed with cancer. She and I made the decision to keep her at home as long as she was comfortable. The last week of her life, I made dozens of trips up the stairs and into her room. Nowa would follow every time I went up, turn around, and go back downstairs. He knew he wasn't allowed in my mother's room.

On the last day of my mother's life, I was very troubled. My father had passed away six years earlier, and now I would face life without either of my parents. I went outside to talk to God. I said, "You know I believe in you and your son, Jesus Christ. But what if this is all there is? What if I never see my mother and father again?"

Very suddenly, a few hours later, the angels came. When my mother was about to take her last breath, I ran for Steven and said, "If you want to be with her, come now." He ran up to my mother's room with Nowa at his heels. As my son entered the room, Nowa attempted to follow. Steven shooed him back with his hand, leaving him in the hallway. As my mother released her last breath a few moments later, Nowa let out a very high-pitched cry from the hallway.

He'd never made a sound like that before and never did again. For me, it was my message. God was telling me that the spiritual world does exist, and Nowa confirmed that he knew my mother's spirit had left her body.

My mother told me before she passed that she'd meet me at the Eastern Gate. Because of this experience, I believe it!

Nowa

Best Friends Animal Society
bestfriends.org

"His home was in my heart"

Linda Schroeder

Turbo had been fighting for his life for eleven years when I met him. He was the runt of a litter of pure-bred Australian Cattle Dogs, and no one wanted him. Then all the wrong families wanted him. He was passed from home to home every year until he reached the age of five. Turbo was the victim of families who liked his looks but didn't understand that an energetic Cattle Dog wasn't the best choice for people who didn't have the space or the time to exercise him.

When I met Turbo, he was with a family with small kids. He would herd them around the house and keep them in corners of rooms. The family was beside themselves, ready to take him to a shelter, when I saw the advertisement asking for yet another home for Turbo.

I'm a dog trainer. I decided to call the family and offer free obedience training in hopes that they'd keep their dog instead of giving him up. They asked me to come. But when I arrived, the family told me they were beyond trying to help Turbo change. They'd given up on him. Because of his personality, I knew he'd be euthanized within days of being surrendered to a shelter, so I put him in my car and left.

Turbo entered a house with ten other dogs; eight were mine, and two were fosters. He hated it. He raged at my other dogs and refused to let me pet him. He wouldn't let any of the other dogs near him. If he was lying on the couch and they came into the room, he would snarl at them. If they were outside and they passed him, he'd attack. He would stay as far away from me and the other dogs as he possibly could. He would even hesitate to eat if I were standing near him. I couldn't even hand him treats. The poor guy was so confused he was lashing out at everyone. I could see his point of view.

Several weeks passed, and there was no change. I decided he needed to see that no harm would come to him if we were close

Turbo

Pilots N Paws
pilotsnpaws.org

together. And so, I tied him to me. He was forced to look at me and react to me on a one-on-one basis. Initially, Turbo would stand at the end of the lead, pulling away from me all the time. He was so spent, so past trusting anyone else. He had had too many homes, and too many people had given up on him. Being tied to him, I began to understand the depth of his pain. And seeing and feeling it taught me patience.

Can you imagine pulling a dog around with you, every minute of the day for days on end? I had to be as stubborn as he was, and that made me laugh at myself. I had never had to work so hard. He was like a rock on the end of a leash, unmoving and unmoved by my distress. My good intentions weren't evident to him, and in spite of all I had to give, I realized he might not want any of it.

Within days of our being tied together, Turbo allowed me to pet him. That was huge. I then decided it was time to take his old collar off and replace it with a new one, with tags. It took a whole afternoon to accomplish. We started outside with meat treats, purchased especially for the task. The meat didn't work to coax him to me. He was not going to be tricked! As I reached for his collar, he tried to warn me by growling and showing his teeth, then tried to bite me. I couldn't get a muzzle on him, so we spent quite a bit of time with me holding him against a fence with my knee, talking to him, calming him, and touching his back and neck. Unfortunately, the new collar was the type you have to slip over the head. There was no quick release. So my hands had to touch his neck and face. He grabbed my hand, and I growled at him and in a low voice told him to drop it. He made the right decision, leaving me with only a couple of small bruises. Once done, that little act turned the tide. With a new collar in place, a new dog emerged. That night, he slept with his head on my pillow and shoulder. He was no longer physically tied to me, but we were forever connected through the heart. I knew he was home.

I have rescued dogs for more than thirty years. Dogs have arrived at my door sick, injured, deformed, old, and scared. Some have been abused. Many have lost their spark of life. All are unwanted. I take the last-chance dogs, the ones who have a history of aggression and are on their way to being euthanized. I take the ones others don't even see. Every dog is different and has its own story.

Turbo was the first dog who made me pause and ask myself if we would ever get past an uneasy truce. He made me work harder to gain his trust than any other dog. Even though I knew his past and how hard it was for him to trust, I questioned whether he would ever "come back" and be "whole" again.

The day Turbo rested his head on my shoulder, I knew he'd started to heal. And he healed all the way. He held nothing back, nothing in reserve. He made a decision to give me his heart and soul, and he never wavered from that, ever. Every night for the next six years, he slept with his head on my shoulder.

When Turbo was eleven, he was diagnosed with stage 3 lymphoma. Nothing could be done. Three veterinarians gave the same time frame; he had four to six weeks to live.

During that time, Turbo had highs and lows. On his low days, he didn't eat. Nothing enticed him. All he could do was look out at the world with sorrowful eyes. I apologized on those days and forced his medication down his throat. I cried and raged at the disease that came without warning. On his high days, Turbo turned into his old self, "Mr. Fun Police!" He wouldn't allow anyone to fetch, run, play, or have any kind of fun at all. He would permit only a certain number of Frisbee throws before he would dash out into the yard, barking and growling, grabbing the Frisbee, and hiding it. It was the same with the ball. He would take his place at the top of the ramp by the door, overlooking his domain, checking to see if anyone else was having fun. If someone was enjoying a stick, he'd take it away and hide it. If someone else was being petted for too long, he'd butt in. And if someone was running through the woods with joy, he'd herd them back into the yard. And the funny thing is, the other dogs all let him do it. On those days, I believed he would live forever. But there was a trend.

When we reached the vet, this little guy who had always needed a double muzzle to enter the vet's office simply allowed me to put him on the table and hold his head gently as the needle was inserted. He watched me the whole time, our eyes inches from each other. He trusted me to do the right thing, even then.

Turbo died with dignity. He was the third of four of my dogs who passed away in a year. My grief was so intense there were times I felt I couldn't breathe. I wanted to empty my life of the pain I experienced with the passing of each dog. Not rescuing one more dog would guarantee that. I went through a period of thinking I would never take another dog into my heart and soul. I wasn't sure I could do rescue anymore. But then I thought about Turbo. The emotions he felt in trusting me were every bit as intense as my pain. He changed. He got through it. The next time I looked into the eyes of a rescue dog, I realized that I'd get through it, too, and would be better for it.

Turbo taught me never to give up on the principles, people, and animals I believe in.

"He'll be waiting for you"

Steve Wood

When I was two years old, I was given a puppy, a Kelpie named Blacky. He quickly became my closest and very best friend. I adored him, and we spent every minute of every day together. He was faithful, loving, and happy.

Blacky slept in the laundry, and each morning, I would rush to him, and we'd play in the backyard until the rest of the family was awake. At breakfast, I'd share my peanut butter toast with him before heading off to school, and during my lunch break, I'd run home to see him. After school, we spent our time together exploring the bushland next to the house until it was time to come inside. The weekends were ours, just the two of us. We were inseparable from dawn to dusk.

When I was eight, my mum came home from the hospital with my newly born younger brother and, sadly, a case of postnatal depression. Blacky happened to jump up on my brother's bassinet, probably to see what all the fuss was about. The next day, Blacky was gone.

I was told he'd been taken to a farm, but I knew, even at eight years old, that he'd probably been put down. It left a very empty space in my heart for a long time.

When I was eighteen, a friend from work told me he had been to a spiritualist meeting held by a group of older ladies at a nearby meeting hall. He'd been impressed by what they'd told them and felt they were genuine and sincere. He suggested I go to a meeting. The concept of communicating with someone who had passed fascinated me, and I decided to go.

I was told I could bring a flower and the ladies would give me a reading from that flower. When they picked my flower, one of the ladies asked me to sit on a chair in the middle of a circle they had formed.

Holding my flower, she looked at me and said, "Dear, you have a very excited dog sitting next to you. You knew him as Blacky, and you were very close. He wants you to know that he'll be waiting for you when you pass over."

I was completely dumbfounded and moved to tears. I'd never told my friend or anyone else at work about my dog Blacky. How could this lady I'd never seen before, who knew nothing about me, tell me something so special?

The experience started me on a quest to learn as much as possible about faith, religion, and spirituality. And at fifty years old, I'm still learning. But from that simple yet profound moment when I was eighteen, I learned that our dogs mean more to us, and we to them, than perhaps we'll ever know.

Dogs' Refuge Home
dogshome.org.au

"She wrote the book
on devotion"

Kay Moore

Meggie was a little Border Collie my family adopted from our local SPCA. When we first saw her, she was cowering in the corner of a pen with her two siblings. She was only ten weeks old, and yet she was terrified of life. On the drive home, she vomited and then spent the afternoon hiding under our couch. We would later learn she hated long sticks, especially canes. This small pup had experienced something horrible, something that would affect her for her entire life. Little did I know, this timid, frightened dog would become a wonderfully loyal companion.

At the time Meggie came into my life, I lived in an all-male house with my husband and two teenage sons. Meggie became my female friend, the one I could talk to, who understood my moods. When I was discouraged, she would get up from wherever she was and come to me. I shared everything with her, and she understood. She was my little girl. And although everyone in the house loved her and treated her amazingly, she was a one-woman dog. She was never on a leash, because she never thought of leaving my side. Meggie wrote the book on devotion.

I live on a fifteen-acre farm in the middle of one of the most beautiful islands in the world, Mount Desert Island, Maine. There is a brook that flows through the center of the property surrounded by fields. Beyond the fields are forty acres of pine trees and woods. This was the world Meggie and I lived in and explored together.

Meggie never barked but was always keenly aware of her surroundings. Without her senses, I would have missed many of life's wonders, such as the day she sat next to me staring in one direction, never moving. When I turned to see what she was focusing on, I watched a mother deer gently help her newly dropped fawn up for the first time.

Our time together was precious and simple. Lying on a granite ledge on a warm autumn day with Meggie made me happy.

In her thirteenth year, it became obvious that Meggie wasn't well. Some say when a person loves their pet, they know when the time is right to release them from this earth. For many years, I trusted Meggie with everything. It was now my turn to return that trust. I made the phone call to our veterinarian, and a time was arranged to end her suffering the next morning.

I wept most of the evening, until it was time to go to bed. Upon retiring, Meggie came to her usual sleeping spot by my side of the bed and lifted her head for her final good-night pat. The fear of her leaving me was unbearable and heartbreaking. How could I do this? How could I get through this? I cried myself to sleep.

I slept fitfully. And then, in the early hours of the morning, my former dog, a Husky named Yuki, came to me in a dream. She came bounding up to me, smiling a big doggie smile. She was overjoyed. I asked her what she was doing there, and she said, "I just came to tell you I'm happy. It's fun here." She told me that once dogs die, they still run and are happy. She told me there was nothing to worry about. I woke up and realized I'd just been visited by Yuki's spirit. No one can convince me otherwise, because it's been a profound and lasting awareness. I remember that morning as if it happened yesterday.

Since that dream, I know that there's a doggie heaven and that Meggie's there. I can't tell you anything about the place, but I know it's real. That special message confirmed to me that just because I'm a human being, I'm not any higher in the spiritual ranks than my beloved pets.

Society for the Prevention of Cruelty to Animals of Hancock County
spcahancockcounty.org

Angel

Guide Dog Foundation for the Blind
guidedog.org

"The more we love, the more we receive"

Troy Wells

My chocolate Labrador, Angel, was a licker. If she had the chance, she would lick my face, my friends' faces, my partner's face, and when my mom came to town, she licked her legs after she got out of the shower. She was a happy licker.

At bedtime, her licking was maternal. She would climb up on the bed and lick my dog Parker's ears until they were clean, as a mother would do for her pups. She would then lick his face.

With Angel, everything was in the moment. Most people need therapy because the past is part of who they are today. I think the whole thing about living in the moment is a spiritual evolution. Angel helped me grow in that respect by showing me that every moment was special.

I had a lifetime of moments with her. When she was happy, I smiled. When she was playful, I laughed. When she sat under my desk with her head resting on my feet, I was loved. And some of my favorite moments were rituals.

Angel had an endless appetite. It seemed as if her food would disappear in one breath. Eating was one of her favorite things to do, and she could barely wait for morning so she could eat. The way she coaxed me to get her breakfast still makes me smile. Angel was always the first to wake up in our bed, or that's what I'd let her think. I would lie in bed limp, and she would try everything to wake me. She would start by breathing in my face. She would move in as close as she could without actually touching me. When that didn't work, she would use her nose to pull my covers off. If that wasn't successful, she'd nudge my arm until it fell off the side of the bed. And if all else failed—and it often did—she'd gently climb up and sit on my torso (all sixty-five pounds of her) and whimper. Joyfully, she indulged me with our morning play, up to and even on the last day of her life.

Angel died suddenly of a brain aneurysm when she was twelve years old.

I think that losing someone dear to our hearts deepens our character profoundly. After losing Angel, I realized that "the moment" is all we are promised, and if we look closely, beauty surrounds us.

After Angel died, I gathered the photos my partner and I had taken of her over the years, with the intention of making an album. But because I was still mourning her loss, I put them away until a later date.

Many months passed, and I found the perfect album. But again, I put it away until the time was right.

One morning, I ran across the photos and spread them out on the breakfast table. I pulled out the photo album and decided this was the day to fill it with happy memories. As I was arranging the photos, from puppy to passing, my partner asked what I was doing. I told him I was making a photo album of Angel. He looked at me quizzically. "Do you know what today is?" I didn't. "Angel passed away one year ago today," he said. That was my first sign.

Years passed, and one morning, I woke up and began sharing a funny dream with my partner. I had dreamed that a dog was licking me all over my face. With a quick response, he reminded me that Angel had passed on the very same day three years before.

Angel's profound reminders of her anniversary have strengthened my faith in the unseen. Most people look for a sign after a loved one passes. I got mine more than once. Some may say it was consciously coincidental, the date locked into my memory banks, but I don't think so. I think we all get signs from our pets when they have passed, but our consumed minds overlook what we might consider a sign. I've decided not to worry about what others think. If you consider it a sign, cradle it in your heart, and know that your little one is always with you.

Angel taught me to focus on the joy and happiness of the moment we are in. My parents are elderly now, and I sometimes think about their passing and what life will be like afterward, but then I remind myself that I can live those moments when they come. Angel taught me to enjoy my parents now.

Angel had a divine purpose in my life. She taught me that the more we love, the more love we receive. The moment is now.

"Life isn't a problem
to be solved"

Tom Sullivan

When my mom was in the final months of her life, my dad was her primary caregiver. I watched as he changed her diapers and eased her pain in every way he could. He loved her unconditionally. I never fully understood the magnitude of what was involved in loving someone that much until Parker, my Weimaraner–Labrador Retriever, was older.

Almost anyone can raise a dog, but I feel God chose my partner and me to raise Parker, to give him the love and security he'd never known, and also to teach us about life. Parker had been abandoned and was found wandering alone in the north Georgia countryside. Initially, he wouldn't even come into the house. But with love and nurturing, he quickly became a member of our family, along with our chocolate Labrador, Angel.

He was named Parker for "keeper of the park," because his favorite thing to do was to go on walks. When we would say, "Parker, wanna go for a walk?" his ears would perk up, he'd tilt his head sideways, and he'd begin to sing. He'd howl, and we'd howl with him. When he wasn't walking, he'd lie on the bed and look out the front window, watching every soul who walked by, keeping a particularly close eye on the neighbor's cat, who liked to hunt in the nearby bushes.

Parker's unconditional love enriched my soul. He was a peaceful rock in my life of transition. When I was laid off from my job of thirty years and then two years later was let go from another job, he was the one who gave me purpose.

I started going to church, where I found a peace that transcended all understanding. It was the same feeling I had with Parker. He was not only my companion, my buddy, and my child but was also a divine soul who understood everything about me.

Thirteen years passed. We lived a blissful life. And then, one morning, Parker yelped as he walked down the back stairs into the yard. His legs were starting to give out. That day, I built him a ramp into the yard and lowered my bed to the floor.

When Parker became incontinent, I learned all about diapers, from sizing to cutting a hole for his tail. I knew that using a diaper would save my sanity from having to mop the floor of urine that flowed at any time of day or night.

As the months ticked by, Parker's arthritis in his rear legs became more pronounced. He started losing body weight, so we fed him bread between meals and sometimes ground beef with his dry food, to encourage his appetite. He hated taking the pills prescribed for his arthritis, so we decided on natural fish oils and glucosamine to help the inflammation in his joints.

In the last two months of Parker's life on the physical plane, I found myself waking up at all hours of the morning to change his diaper and take him outside. I would sleep in three-hour segments, then wake to comfort him. One morning at four, with little sleep, I cried out to God, saying, "I can't do this anymore. Please take him in his sleep." I didn't want to play God. I didn't want to make the decision to end his life. I hoped God would make it easy for me. But I also knew that God wanted me to take care of him until the very last moment.

My friends kept saying, "You'll know when it's time," or "God will give you a sign." And they were right. One morning, I woke to take him outside. I'd noticed earlier that week that he was walking slightly crooked. This morning, he could barely stand and al-

Tom and Parker

Pets Are Loving Support
palsatlanta.org

most fell trying to reach the back door. At that moment, I knew. I e-mailed Dr. McReynolds, a local vet who made house calls, and asked her to call me in the morning.

Parker went to his bed in the living room, where he sometimes stayed after getting up early, and I crawled back into bed and stared at the ceiling, thinking of my decision. A few hours later, I woke to the sound of Parker whimpering. His diaper had fallen off. He had defecated on his bed, gotten up, walked two feet, urinated, and then slipped and fell on the hardwood floors. I burst into tears, helped him up, massaged his legs, and told my partner about the decision I'd made earlier in the morning.

At noon, I phoned Dr. Reynolds. "How about three o'clock?" she asked. "That will give you some time with Parker."

I had just three hours left with my baby here on earth. Every emotion ran through my body. God had given us a beautiful day filled with warm sunshine, blue skies, and butterflies enjoying the flowers. My partner and I tried to hide our emotions so he wouldn't pick up on the sadness. We took pictures and a video and helped him take his favorite walk down the street. When we returned home, Parker slowly waddled up the ramp to the house, drank some water, and went to his bed. I fed him pieces of roast beef from my hands. Feeling the warmth of his nose and tongue on my fingers was comforting. I kept looking at my watch, knowing that soon my buddy would be pain-free and on his way to running and playing with his sister Angel, who had left three and a half years before.

A little before three, Dr. McReynolds arrived. She knelt down and loved on Parker, rubbing his head and giving him warm kisses. He didn't seem to mind her presence as he did with most people. Perhaps he knew she was going to help him. Perhaps the peace he was feeling was because he knew God was right there with him.

The house was quiet and serene. A soft, warm breeze floated through the open windows. While Dr. McReynolds prepared to release Parker to heaven, we listened to a song that reminded us of Parker's love and grace. As the song played, Parker drifted off into a deep sleep, leaving his pain and suffering behind. A short time later, the warmth of his nose was gone, and his spirit was free of his aging vehicle.

Later that night, we received a gift. The house was still. All of a sudden, we heard the sound of toenails clicking up and down the hardwood floors. Both of us sat upright. We both heard it. And then, a bit later, I heard Parker shake his head and the flapping of his soft silver-gray ears along with the jingle of his collar—the same sound I heard every day when he awoke. The sound gave me the chills. I got up to investigate. And even though I couldn't see Parker, I could feel his presence. His spirit was alive and sending me a sign that he was fine. He didn't want me to be sad. He would be waiting for me with our dog Angel at the gates of heaven, when it was time.

Parker is a divine creation, an extension of God. Through him, I learned how to love unconditionally. Parker also taught me that life isn't a problem to be solved. It's a divine mystery to be experienced.

It wasn't until I was personally involved in caretaking for Parker that I fully understood what my father had done for my mother. He had loved her unconditionally. That's when I called my dad and thanked him for everything he did for my mom. And that's when, for the first time, I told my father I loved him.

"I am not afraid of dying now"

Sally Nicholson-Fisher

Billy was five years old when I found him at the Retired Grey-hound Trust (RGT) in Essex, England. The RGT is a charity that rehomes retired Greyhounds. I went to its kennels for a visit, never intending to come home with a dog. But I fell in love with a very large black-and-white Greyhound named Billy. I was told Billy had been a champion hurdler on the racetrack before he was retired, and he was professionally known as "Wood Cherish."

The first day I brought him home, he wandered around, in-specting the premises, and then he suddenly hopped over the sofa. It was obvious he was a hurdling champion.

The dog was beautiful in motion. He was also extremely intel-ligent and very loving. Being with him made me happy. He adored me, and I him. We soon had rituals we both enjoyed. Every night after work, we would take a walk together. His favorite place was a local spot called Hilly Fields, where he could run in a huge field. On weekends, we spoiled ourselves and went to a wildlife park called Whitewebbs in Enfield, where there was a lot of open space. Billy was free to hurdle over logs in the forest and run through fields and alongside the river. Watching him run was joy. He was like liquid sunlight, sleek and beautiful, a furry rocket.

Our time together was beautiful and fun. Billy could make me laugh. One memory still makes me smile. Once a year, the RGT was permitted to hold a fundraising event at Walthamstow Racing Stadium, as many of its dogs ended up at the RGT kennels. The event involved many of the old dogs wearing coats with their racing names on them and being paraded, with their proud owners, around the track. The track was slightly raised above the heads of the spectators. At one of the events, Billy lifted his leg and peed over the crowd. He scored a bull's-eye on one man, who roared with laughter, as did his friends. I wondered if he was showing contempt for the "sport" that had discarded him once his winning days were over. But it was a good day. People were pointing at Billy and saying, "There's old Wood Cherish. He made me a few bob!" I couldn't help but hope they'd give something back by donating to the RGT.

Billy was with me for five short years. There came a time when his character changed, and he started snapping at people. Then he began to bite. It broke my heart to think people were scared of him or referred to him as vicious. So I took Billy to the veterinarian, hoping that perhaps he had an ache that was making him grumpy. The news was worse. Billy had a brain tumor, and it had been changing his personality. I took him home and prepared for the terrible day when I'd say my final good-bye.

On that morning, my son George and I took him to his favorite place, Hilly Fields, for one last run. That night, we took him to the vet. And as I sat on the floor holding Billy, the soul who had given me the love that no male partner had ever shown me, my heart broke.

Some months later, I visited a spiritualist. She knew nothing of me. As I sat down, before she said anything else, she said, "There is a large dog sitting next to you."

I couldn't believe it. She knew absolutely nothing about me.

That was confirmation that he's still with me and always will be. I'm not afraid of dying now. I'm absolutely clear that I'll meet Billy again. Love never dies—at least, not the love between a dog and a committed owner.

Retired Greyhound Trust
retiredgreyhounds.co.uk

Peanut

Chihuahua Rescue and Transport
chihuahua-rescue.com

"She was the child I chose"

Elaine Smothers

The day I'd refused to acknowledge had arrived. The cancer had spread throughout Peanut's ravaged body. Her organs were shutting down, first her kidneys, then her liver. The only thing she'd eaten in two days was a few teaspoons of baby food, just enough to let me know she refused to give up. I knew she'd never stop fighting, for although I'd told her it was okay to leave, she knew I wasn't ready to accept it. Peanut, my frail, cancer-riddled, sixteen-year-old Chihuahua, wasn't just my best friend for sixteen years. She was my teacher, my mentor, and my confidante.

When Peanut came into my life as a seven-week-old pup, I had just married, and she was the "child" I chose. In hindsight, I could not have chosen better. Through thirteen years of an abusive marriage, two years of caretaking for a terminally ill parent, a bitter divorce, and four years of life alone, she kept me sane. She taught me the true meaning of unconditional love, the importance of boundaries, the sacredness of trust and loyalty, and the unbridled joy of living in the moment. But her greatest gift and lesson would break the veil between life on this side and life on the other.

Several weeks in advance, I'd made arrangements with the vet to allow Peanut to pass at home. She'd always been terrified of the vet's office, and I was determined that she would leave this life surrounded by the people and things she loved most. So, on a cold February morning, when her suffering became too great, I made the dreaded call.

A day later, Peanut lay in my lap with her head across my arm, her gentle kisses still trying to comfort me. Her frail, emaciated frame seemed almost weightless, and she offered no objections as the vet inserted the butterfly IV into her leg. As she took her final shallow breath, the thread that bound her to this life was broken. The weight of her gently settled into my arms, free of pain and suffering and in peace at last. My heart was broken.

I covered her rapidly cooling body with a blanket and placed her in her favorite bed. I couldn't bear to let the vet take her body; I couldn't part with what little remained of her that soon. So I sat with her for several hours, wondering how I'd survive this final loss and questioning whether I even wanted to. I took her remains to the vet's office that evening to be delivered to the crematorium the next day. I don't even remember the drive home, but I distinctly remember the empty, tomblike feel of my apartment when I arrived. Where once there had been joyous tail wagging and kisses of elation, there was only emptiness and a dead, pervasive silence that was deafening. I couldn't bring myself to pack up her food and water bowls or her bed and toys, so I left them in their rightful place as if she might return. I was a long way from acceptance and past the point of even caring. She was gone, I was alone, and there was nothing left that seemed to matter.

I ran a tub of water so hot the sweat poured from my body as hard and fast as the tears from my eyes. As I stared at the ceiling and listened for the familiar pitter-patter of tiny toenails on linoleum, words and then sentences began to arrange and rearrange themselves and take shape in my mind. I hadn't written poetry in years. Not since the loss of my mother to a similar cancer almost ten years and one month to the day. Yet the process felt eerily familiar, as one sentence flowed into another until the poem was complete. I hurriedly dried off, dressed, and rushed to the computer to write it down in its entirety before it could evaporate like steam from the rapidly cooling bath water.

It wasn't yet dark, but I went to bed anyway. There would be little sleep that night. It didn't help that her favorite place was under the comforter by my side with her head on my arm. Her absence was palpable and sleep fitful at best. I spent the next day in a well of grief and depression so dark and deep it seemed bottomless. I was physically and emotionally exhausted and spent the day alternating between bouts of crying and short-lived naps on the couch. I looked through old pictures, ran my hands over the toys she treasured, and stretched out on the bed she loved to sun herself in. I couldn't grasp the permanence of it, the idea that she was gone and wouldn't be coming back.

Shortly after midnight, I turned on the computer and connected to the Internet. I visited Web sites devoted to pet loss, rereading the story of the Rainbow Bridge, and posted several online memorials to her. I halfheartedly participated in a few discussions in one of the pet-loss chat rooms but mostly read other stories similar to my own. It helped to know I wasn't the only one feeling such deep loss and devastation. Across the miles, a group of strangers with a common bond united in their grief and sorrow for friends lost and lovingly remembered.

I stared at the four walls of my empty apartment and knew I had two options: end it now, or find a reason to get out of bed every morning and go on with life. I had no close family or siblings, and the second option would require another living being. I couldn't imagine looking for another dog this soon. It made me feel shameful and traitorous to her memory. Still, I forced myself to scroll through page after page of available dogs on Petfinder and the classifieds to gauge my reaction. Nothing. No interest.

It was close to 2 A.M. when I stepped outside the house to get some fresh air. The fluorescent lights in the breezeway cast enough light into the backyard to see Peanut's favorite sunning and potty-break spots. It was bitterly cold, the kind of weather neither of us liked. The stars were like frozen crystals embedded in a black granite sky. About fifteen yards from the breezeway, a small knoll edged the grassy area and steeply dropped away into a thickly wooded ravine that bordered a neighboring subdivision. The ground beneath was covered in a deep layer of dead leaves that made even the furtive movements of a squirrel impossibly loud for an animal its size. As my gaze came to rest on the knoll, a small tan animal with large ears appeared on the crest. It sat down and looked directly at me. It had to have come up the ravine from the wooded area, yet there'd been no sound, and the ground cover precluded that possibility. The hair on my arms stood up as I tried to convince myself that there was a logical explanation for what I saw. It soon became apparent that she wasn't of this world and my rationalizations were pointless. It looked like Peanut in the prime of her life, young again and in good health. Her gaze never left me, nor mine on her, for close to five minutes. She was as motionless as the sentinel trees behind her, no shivering and no shaking, although I was doing plenty for both of us. When I made an attempt to approach, she disappeared as silently as she'd come.

I didn't realize how hard I was trembling or that the tears were running down my face until I closed the door behind me. I sat on the sofa and stared out the window, at the area where she'd appeared. I didn't expect her to return again, and she didn't. But I couldn't stop trying to rationalize the experience and explain it away as a chance encounter or random coincidence. When I looked down and realized the hair on my arms was still standing on end, I stopped looking for explanations and let the joy of the moment wash over me. I remembered how Peanut had always managed to find the joy in every minute God gave her. And with her last breath, she was licking, consoling, and comforting me when it must have taken all the strength her tiny body had to offer.

I sat down at the computer and stared at the screen. I marveled at the miracle that was dog and wondered how I could best honor her memory. When I'd gotten up to walk outside, I'd left the computer on a page of Chihuahua listings. I went to the next page, and the face of two tiny angels appeared, two little Chihuahua sisters I somehow already knew. Their names were Hope and Grace. There was never any doubt; it was a deep and instant knowing of the kind you don't question. Perhaps I had the life of one more dog in me, so why not two at once? What better way to honor Peanut's memory than to give the last of my love to another? Was that what Peanut came back to tell me? I believe it was. She'd found a way to bring me the faith in knowing we would be together again someday . . . and the Hope and Grace to see me through.

Memories bring back younger years before age took away
all the things you loved to do; to jump, to run, to play,
to lie on sun-baked concrete, on the hearth before the fire,
to snuggle under covers and freshly dried attire.
In times of joy and sorrow, sickness and despair,
my world was always brighter just for your being there.
But now as your body fails you, age has brought us to a place
where death stands by in waiting; no final saving grace.
As I hold you for the last time, even unto death,
you lick my tears, console me, until your final breath.
Yet I still feel you with me; I know we'll never part
for you live on inside of me, you're buried in my heart.

Compassion

Understanding with Empathy

S ome people believe dogs aren't capable of compassion. If you've known the love of a dog, you know that's just not true. According to professor and scientist Marc Bekoff, dogs have empathy and compassion toward others and experience emotions and feelings. Bekoff is a leader in the study of animals' minds. In his book *The Emotional Lives of Animals*, he backs up his work with references to more than two hundred scientific journals, papers, and books. He notes that neurological and behavioral studies have consistently shown that our fellow animals experience emotions including fear, anger, sadness, and joy. Bekoff and other experts are unlocking the mystery by scientifically confirming what most of us know: dogs care.

Surely, many of us have experienced compassion from dogs, especially when we're upset. This morning, after a week of watching my darling dog ChickPea suffer with paralysis from a brain tumor, I found myself crumpled on the floor sobbing, fearing the inevitable. Her best mate, CousCous, who hadn't left ChickPea's side for days and could barely walk herself, came to me, found her way to my face, and licked me energetically. I could almost hear her saying, "I feel for you, but knock it off. I need to get back to her." If you've known the love of a dog, this isn't surprising, and you've probably experienced something similar.

One of the funniest stories I know about dogs and empathy I learned while on an expedition to London. At the time, I was serving on the Committee (Board of Directors) at the Dogs' Refuge Home in Perth, Australia. Our rehoming goal, like that of all rescues, was to find the perfect homes for our dogs—the first time, to avoid a cycle of abandonment. To explain this further, think of the child who spends his life going from foster home to foster home. He often grows up with abandonment issues. The same thing happens to dogs. Dogs want love and the security that comes with it—like all of us. So, we strive to match the adopter with the dog that's perfect for him and his lifestyle. It's not easy. When I heard that the Battersea Dogs and Cats Home was using a software program that helped weed out potential matching problems, I happily took a field trip to London.

Battersea Dogs and Cats Home was established in 1860 and is the oldest home for displaced pets in London. Today it's a well-endowed organization that focuses on finding good homes for more than ten thousand animals a year.

The charity embraced my interest and invited me to shadow the staff. After getting a behind-the-scenes tour of the facility, I was assigned to a young lady to learn about rehoming. The waiting room was full of people waiting to adopt. I was seated in the back of a small, glassed-in interview room while applicants came in and were interviewed. Their answers were put into a computer program, and the computer matched them with the perfect dog or dogs for them. Little did I know just how well the system worked until an older mother and daughter entered the room with their dog.

Immediately, their stench overwhelmed me. The mother was in her seventies and her daughter in her fifties. They were unkempt in appearance and clearly hadn't bathed in a long time. Their large dog, a Spaniel, was happy and clearly adored them. They explained that they had recently lost his pal to old age and were seeking a companion for him. They also said they had cats.

Battersea has as many as four hundred dogs at its facility at any given moment. The interviewer put the ladies' details into the computer, and only two matches came up. One of those matches, she explained to them, was a white, pure-bred Scottish Terrier. The ladies were excited. "But," the interviewer said, "he has behavioral issues." She carefully explained that he had been rehomed three times and had been brought back each time. He was a good boy but marked. I thought to myself, "Well, that's it. Who's going to take a dog they know will pee all over their house?" The ladies looked at each other and shrugged their shoulders, and then the daughter said, "Everyone does that in our house."

A meet-and-greet was organized with their dog. The two got along just fine. And then there was the cat test, an introduction to a cat to see if the dog was reactionary. We all went into a room where a cat had been placed in a travel kennel. The dog had absolutely no interest in that cat. Instead, he lifted his leg on every corner of the room. There was pee everywhere.

The ladies were giddy with excitement that the dog passed the cat and dog tests. As they walked out with their dogs, I had no doubt they'd all live happily together for the rest of their lives.

I was dumbfounded by the experience and was pretty giddy myself. The interviewer and I couldn't stop laughing. We were laughing at the absolute perfection of the match. At the same time, I commended her for not discriminating against people because of their looks or, in this case, smells. I liked her compassion for them. But she explained that compassion and humanity didn't have anything to do with it. It was a computer match. That's when she said, "If you're interested in a story about compassion, I've got one for you. It's about one of our dogs."

It was 2004, and the home was experiencing a series of what it suspected were break-ins. Some of the dogs in one kennel section were repeatedly being let out of their kennels at night. At first, it was suspected that someone was playing a joke. But it happened night after night. Staff arrived in the morning to a messy kitchen and dogs roaming the halls.

Cameras were installed to try to catch the culprit in the act. And they did. It was a guy named Red, a Greyhound-looking mixed breed known as a Lurcher, and he wasn't breaking in, he was breaking out.

As the cameras rolled, Red unbolted his kennel using his nose and teeth and proceeded to the kitchen for a bite to eat. After he'd opened a bag of food and had a meal, he unlocked the kennel of his best friend, the dog he'd been found with. He then released his favorite playmates. A party ensued. There was a feast and lots of playing around. It was the same kind of bash we'd all have if we were imprisoned and had been let out.

Lucky for all of us, Red's escape and compassion for his friends were documented on camera and have been posted on the Internet (YouTube/Intelligent Dog). It's hysterical to watch. It's also proof that dogs care about one another.

I've always been a bit of a dog "nutter." I suspect that because of my close bonds with dogs, a lot of people don't "get" me. But what scientific research combined with my own experience has taught me is that the dogs who have chosen me and whom I have chosen have not only loved me, they've cared about me. And that, I suggest, is one of the reasons our love for dogs surpasses that of most others.

Battersea Dogs and Cats Home
battersea.org.uk

"I couldn't believe it!"

Diane Smith

Running a therapy dog program wasn't something I planned. It started by chance and picked up momentum like a snowball careening down a hill. The originator of all the good energy was a little Beagle, a therapy dog, who visited my grandmom Greth at the Lutheran Home, a retirement community and facility for the elderly. I still don't remember the dog's name, but I remember his personality and how it affected my beloved grandmom.

The Lutheran Home was cheerful when you first got there. It was beautifully appointed, with pretty carpeting, a mahogany side table with fresh flowers at the entrance, and enthusiastic employees wearing chef-style pants greeting you as you entered. It even smelled pretty good. Residents had cute apartments with little gardens on the first floor, some with bird feeders, where couples grew old together. Grandmom had lived there for a few years after my grandpop died and before she was diagnosed with Alzheimer's and dementia.

As residents grew older and their health demanded more attention, they were moved to rooms on the upper floors. I remember

Grandmom crying when she found out she was being sent up. It was scary for her. I also remember thinking I didn't want her to live up there. It was a progression, and I didn't want to lose her anytime soon.

To visit Grandmom's new floor, visitors had to be buzzed in. If you had a room there, you had to wear a hospital-type bracelet that would cause alarms to blare if you wandered toward the elevators. I heard them go off many times. The nurses and staff were wonderful, and the rooms were always clean. But it didn't smell as good as downstairs. There wasn't carpeting, and it looked like a hospital. Residents in wheelchairs hung out in the halls, muttering to themselves or talking to long-departed spouses. Room doors were left open for all to see, and everyone had a roommate.

We visited Grandmom a lot. My sister, my mom, and I would bring the kids over when they were young. We brought pumpkins to carve (a disaster but fun), Halloween decorations, homemade soups, Christmas gifts, and anything else permitted on her floor. We made her a picture book with names of our spouses, children, friends, and anything else that would bring her joy.

The afternoon I met the Beagle, her room was sunny, and it looked better than usual. Grandmom was in her wheelchair, wearing her favorite sweater. Her face was a blank stare as I entered in a flurry with my three year-old daughter, Casey. We were always toting dolls, hats, purses, crayons, and snacks and moved a lot faster than anyone else on that floor, until we got settled in.

A quiet voice preceded the sight of a brown, black, white, and very wiggly Beagle at the entrance to the room. "Is it okay if we visit?" the dog's handler asked. With equal enthusiasm, Casey and I invited them in. I had thought that only family, staff, and clergy were allowed upstairs. This was a great surprise.

Grandmom didn't seem to notice. She lived in her own world, rarely coming out of her haze to remember the past. The Beagle perched himself on her bed, directly across from her as she sat in the wheelchair. He was at eye level with her. All of a sudden, my grandmom lifted her hand and started petting him. She started to come alive. As she stroked him, she started talking. She was talking, asking questions, and making sense. I had only seen this level of awareness fleetingly, when family members visited. This dog had brought that delightful, fun lady back, if only for a little while. I couldn't believe it!

I was never lucky enough to be there on a day when the pet therapy teams came again. But that little Beagle remained a warm memory of a wonderful afternoon with my grandmom and my daughter.

After Grandmom passed, my family adopted Roxy, a gentle-mannered Boykin Spaniel. Roxy had a wonderful disposition. I couldn't help but think she would be a perfect therapy dog. I knew she could help others, and I wanted to be a part of that. We began by practicing for our therapy team evaluation by working with children in a reading-support class. The children found it easier to read aloud to Roxy than to their teachers. I watched each week as Roxy settled into the laps of the children, connecting with them and positively influencing their reading skills.

Six years ago, I founded Roxy Reading Therapy Dogs, a nonprofit, all-volunteer organization. Today, fifty Roxy Reading pet therapy teams are dedicated to promoting literacy, educating our community, and bringing comfort to elementary-school children through visits with their dogs. More than a thousand students have participated in the Roxy Reading program, with weekly visits to more than one hundred classrooms each school year. Our therapy dog teams provide support and unconditional love to children with academic challenges and other serious physical and psychological challenges. Roxy Reading, like so many other wonderful dog programs in the world, began because one compassionate person and her dog took a moment to be kind to an elderly woman on her final journey.

I still visit the class where Roxy and I made our debut, when we were practicing for our therapy test. Sometimes, when we're all spread out on pillows on the floor listening to a child read to Roxy and the sun spills in, I think of Grandmom and that little Beagle. I'm sure that wherever she is, she's listening to our young friend read and offering her encouragement, right along with us.

Roxy

Roxy Reading Therapy Dogs
roxyreading.org

"She always checked on the gravesite"

Linda Pugh

Sheba came from a shelter at the age of six months. When I saw the young black Labrador Retriever in the cage, she was very distressed, with her tail glued to her tummy. I took her home to introduce her to my Lab, Sarah, to see if she would come out of her shell. The two got on like a house on fire. Of course, she stayed and always seemed grateful that my family adopted her.

Soon Sheba and I were attached at the hip. She followed me everywhere and wanted nothing more than to be with me. In the winter, we traveled from our home in Ontario, Canada, to North Myrtle Beach, South Carolina. We lived two minutes from the beach where Sheba and I loved to walk. I would look for shells and shark teeth while she amused herself with seaweed and smelly things. One winter day, as we walked down the deserted beach, Sheba came across a dead seagull. She walked over to it and immediately began burying it with sand, but she didn't use her paws. Instead, she pushed the sand up over the gull with her nose. When

I saw what she was doing, I helped her. When the job was done to her satisfaction, and the gull was completely covered, we went on our way. The next day, she remembered the spot, even though there were no obvious landmarks and we had already walked for miles. She ran up to it and pushed more sand over the little mound. For days after that, she always checked on the gravesite and added more sand if it was necessary.

This compassionate behavior carried over to every other dead animal she came across. One day, I found her pushing cedar chips over a dead mouse. Another time, I witnessed her pushing pieces of gravel from the driveway over a dead snake. It bothered me that she used her nose for these burials, because she sometimes suffered cuts as a result. But that didn't deter her. Year after year, I witnessed her thoughtfulness. Each time I watched her bury a dead animal, it gave me goose bumps. I cried to think she cared so much about another creature.

I should mention, in case you think she may have been stashing these creatures for future consumption, that she has buried bones in the veggie garden, but for this task, she always used her feet. She also had a surprising mean streak. If my husband was sitting in his beach chair on the sand, she loved to excavate a huge hole close to the back legs of the chair. Inevitably, he would capsize into the hole. Again, she always used her feet to play her tricks.

I had eleven wonderful years with my soul mate. Sheba taught me that every morning is like Christmas morning, something to get excited about. And every car trip is an adventure, where the driver must be licked on the ear from the backseat. She showed me how to enjoy the simple things in life: lazing in the sun, sniffing the air, rolling in the grass, going for a long walk, or just hanging out with your best friend.

There was one more thing I learned from Sheba. The dead should be buried, not tossed into the compost. I was amazed that Sheba had compassion for animals of other species. Now when I find a dead bird that has flown into a window or drowned in the pond, I bury it. That's what Sheba would want me to do.

Sheba

Franklin County Humane Society
franklincountyhumanesociety.org

Bella

PJ's Pals
pjspals.org

"I could see him in the shadows, sobbing"

Debbie Harrie

My Australian Shepherd Blue Merle, named Bella, came into my life at one of my loneliest times. I had lost two of my best friends within three months of each other. My girlfriend died instantly in a car accident after leaving my house just before Christmas, and my dog of thirteen years, Bandit, lost her battle with cancer shortly after that.

Unbeknownst to me, my husband, Tom, began searching for an Australian Shepherd puppy in hopes of lifting my spirits. He enlisted the help of our veterinarian, who located a puppy at a breeder, the last one in a litter of ten. My husband was thrilled. I wasn't. When he told me his plan, I told him I didn't want a puppy.

I didn't want to open myself up to love and care about something that could be taken away. I didn't feel that Bandit could be replaced, and I didn't want someone to try to replace her in my life. I was lost, lonely, and angry. I now knew that someone I loved could be by my side one moment and gone the next. I wasn't ready to move forward.

Still, Tom persuaded me to go to the breeder's house to have a look at the puppies. As I stood there, reluctantly looking at the ten pups, the smallest of the litter, the runt, crawled over the other puppies and came to us. The breeder picked her up and gave her to me. The puppy snuggled into me. I held her for a minute and then gave her to my husband. We left without making a commitment. But I couldn't get her off my mind. When I had held her so close to my heart, she had touched me, and I realized I couldn't keep up the wall.

Bella was eight weeks old when we brought her home. She was a small bundle of white, brown, black, and blue fluff, with one brown eye and a brown/light blue eye. She was a Merle, which means "marble of colors." I knew immediately that she was a gift from God, and I was thankful.

Three months later, we were at home on a Sunday evening. Tom and I live in the Mojave Desert in California, at the base of a rock outcropping. We were getting ready to have a late dinner, and we took Bella out to go to the bathroom. She began her investigation in the yard, and there was a scream like I've never heard before. My husband ran to her and saw she had been bitten on the face by a rattlesnake. Tom grabbed a shovel and killed the snake, knowing we needed to bring it to the veterinarian with us. It would be important to know what type of rattlesnake it was to determine the type of antivenom that needed to be used to try to save Bella's life.

Looking at the snake, you could see it had just eaten a rodent. Luckily, it had expelled its venom on its previous victim. According to our vet, Bella had received a dry bite. He told us that if it hadn't been a dry bite, tiny Bella would not have survived the trip to his office. It was at that moment I decided she was a gift that I had to share. I set a goal. Together we would provide therapy for others.

In the summer of 2010, Bella and I were asked to attend a bereavement camp for children who had lost someone special. It was our first time, and I was apprehensive. I kept telling myself that Bella would know what to do. I'm not sure I totally believed it, but I knew she had the potential. We would be there for the children if they needed a soft, fuzzy friend.

It was a nice day. Bella enjoyed interacting with the kids. She received lots of pets, entertained with tricks, and even went swimming with the kids.

During the day, the children decorated brown waxed-paper bags to represent their love for the person they had lost. A candle was placed in each bag. As the day turned to dusk, the children gathered at the lake and placed their bags on a raft. Some spoke about the person they loved. When darkness came, the candles were lit, and the raft was gently released on the lake.

There was a lot of emotion around us. Bella felt it and didn't like it. She let out a low, long cry. I thought that if she continued crying, I would have to leave. I reached down and explained to her that it was okay.

A lady from the program came to me and asked if we could walk past a young boy who was filled with grief. I could see him in the shadows, sobbing. This was why we had come. I gathered Bella's blanket and water and my bag and walked over to where I'd seen the boy. But he was gone. I felt horrible. Bella and I looked and looked for him. It was dark, and we were in a forested area. Finally, I had to give up. It had been the one thing we had been asked to do all day, and we had failed.

I spoke to Bella, saying, "We tried our best, but we just can't find him. We have to go back." But she didn't want to turn around. I decided to let her lead. She wanted to walk to the other side of the lake, to the people there. I just let her go. Along the way, she found some large boulders and climbed them. I had to go around. When I reached the other side, there was Bella in the moonlight, standing behind a young boy.

She didn't make a sound and waited until he realized she was there. I watched as he moved his things for her. She immediately stepped forward to be next to him. The scene was stunning—a young boy and a dog sitting on a boulder overlooking a peaceful lake, their heads lit by a full moon. I watched silently as they talked and then noticed the boy's posture change. He seemed to be doing better. At that point, Bella stood up.

I approached and told the boy that Bella was very happy and had appreciated his petting. He smiled and said, "She's very welcome." We said good-bye, and Bella climbed back down the boulder the same way she'd come up. As we walked away, her head was up, her shoulders back, she was smiling, and her butt was wiggling with satisfaction.

A few minutes later, the lady who'd asked for our help approached us. She thanked us for finding the boy and talking to him. I realized that Bella had actually found the boy who needed our help. I'd given up hope that we would find him. Bella didn't. It was the most profound moment in my life. I looked down at my happy dog and felt overwhelmed with love. I couldn't believe what she'd done. I had just witnessed something extraordinary between a dog and a child who didn't know each other. It made me realize that there must be a higher power for something so extraordinary to have happened.

As we prepared to go home, Bella saw another little boy. He was crying as he walked alone, holding a tissue tightly. She moved quickly to catch up. Once beside him, she put her head under his small hand. He stopped, and they talked, and he gave her a big hug. As he walked away, he put his tissue in his pocket. That is how our evening at that special camp ended.

I now believe that when we think something is impossible, it's not. Bella inspires me to be a better person and to give for no reason except for the joy of helping others. I feel grateful and blessed every time I look at her. One of the most important things I've learned from Bella is that we're not always meant to lead. Sometimes we should just follow and have faith in where we're being taken.

"His head was buried in her fur"

Alice Kugelman

In 1994, I founded Connecticut Canine Search & Rescue, a team of professionally trained volunteers who search for people who are lost, missing, or drowned. The team is made up of a dozen dogs and their handlers. Each dog has trained for a year and a half before it's allowed to participate in a search. Each handler has trained for two years.

One of our very first call-outs was to search for a young man believed to have committed suicide. He was missing in western Connecticut. The local fire chief deployed us, and the state police assigned us to search a heavily wooded area, not far from where the man's pickup truck was found.

On the first day, we used a topographical map to come up with a search plan, dividing the area into sectors of up to forty acres each. Teams consisting of a handler, a dog, and a Search & Rescue teammate were assigned to different areas. My team, including my Newfoundland, Juno, searched the woods for several hours and found nothing on the first day.

On the second day of the search, I was assigned to radio communications and remained at the base camp that was set up, just off the road near the missing man's truck. Teams dispersed into the woods, and many hours passed before the call came in from one of the teams reporting a "find."

In Search & Rescue, those who make the find are required to remain in place until law enforcement can take over the scene. In this case, the team was in a remote part of the woods, approximately three-quarters of a mile from base. These were the days before GPS was used. It took a long time for help to arrive.

Shortly after news of the find went across the scanner, friends of the deceased began showing up at our base camp. At that time, everything became more stressful, because part of our job was to keep them at base and away from the actual scene of the death.

At the base was a clearing where an old church had once stood. All that was left were the remnants of a stone foundation. While I was working radio communications, I looked over at the foundation, and saw a scene that's permanently etched in my memory.

A young man, obviously a friend of the victim, was sitting on the stone foundation of the church. One of our dogs, Abbey, a Golden Retriever, was sitting in front of him, facing him. The man's arms were wrapped around the dog, and his head was buried in her fur.

This gentle dog was reading emotions and knew where to go to offer her help in calming the crisis.

A few years later, another Golden was involved in a water search for a drowning victim. As the inflatable boat the dog was in landed on the beach where people were waiting for news, he jumped from the boat and immediately targeted a woman sitting in a folding chair. He went up to her and buried his head in her lap. She was the wife of the man who had drowned.

This scenario has been repeated many times in the fifteen years since that Golden, unbidden, taught me that many dogs know who needs solace.

Connecticut Canine Search and Rescue

ccsar.org

"I prayed for someone to help me through my grief"

David Holmes

It was December 17, 2005. I had just celebrated my best friend John's fifty-first birthday a few days before when I received a call from his sister, Barbara. She was worried about him. No one had heard from him in two days. I knew John well enough to know that after his party, he was probably taking a few days off. I didn't feel the urgency. I begrudgingly agreed to meet her at his house.

I walked into John's bedroom, and at first, it looked as if he was asleep. But he wasn't. He would never wake up again.

In times like these, you truly return to the God of your childhood. I began to pray. I prayed for understanding. I prayed for peace. I prayed that someone would understand my grief.

In the harried days and weeks that followed, with the funeral and meetings with family and friends, I noticed my dog, Buster (a very good-looking ugly duckling sort of Rat Terrier mixed breed), was more attentive to me than usual. He was always at my side and in need of a pet on the head. I thought little of it until one morning when all of the stress of the death and the funeral culminated in a big breakdown, and I cried as I hadn't since my grandmother had passed some twenty years before.

I prayed, once more, for someone to help me through my grief. As I continued to pray, I noticed that Buster was whimpering and pacing around on the floor. It was silly of me, but I thought he just wanted to go for a walk. Finally, Buster left the room and came back carrying his tennis ball in his mouth. He slowly walked to my chair and, with his nose, pushed the ball under my leg. He then turned around, walked over to his bed, and lay down. That's when it dawned on me. This was the sweetest, most generous act Buster could think

Buster

Pets Are Loving Support
palsatlanta.org

of. He had given me his most cherished possession. It was as if he was saying, "Take this ball. It always makes me feel better."

Buster's gift yanked me out of uncontrollable grief. He helped me realize that he wasn't just my dog. But I was also his human. Since I'd rescued him at a Humane Society two years before, I'd thought I was doing him a favor by taking him on regular walks, having play time, and making sure he was fed and comfortable. I had never thought that he also played a very important role in my life and that, in his mind, perhaps he felt he was there for me, too.

I am grateful to God for Buster, who was by my side on that terrible day. I now know that the people and animals in my life will help me get through anything, no matter how difficult. The biggest lesson I've learned is that God brought Buster and me together to be here for each other. And we are.

People tell me they're very proud of me for "rescuing" Buster, but I think who rescued whom is the real question.

"She refused to leave me"

Lori Hoffman

It was an ordinary morning in March 2001. Little did I know that on this day, my life would change forever.

At 8 A.M., I was driving the usual route to work in Tampa, Florida, when I turned onto a desolate back road. The road runs through a remote area and is known as a place where people dump dogs, cats, and other unwanted animals. I always took this route to see if anyone needed my help. In this area, there is no hope of survival for an abandoned animal. The single-lane, winding road is bordered on both sides by ditches with thick, tall grasses and scrub trees. Animals often suffer horrible death from starvation, are hit by cars, or are consumed by alligators as they try to drink from water pits.

After making the turn, I came upon three German Shepherds, obviously deserted.

I stopped and got out of my car. It was evident that all three dogs were female and had been used for breeding. They were extremely thin and had fear in their eyes. They were all skittish in my presence, most likely having never known human affection.

I desperately wanted to help them. I planned to return that evening after work with food.

At 6:30 P.M., I returned with a huge box of packaged frozen cheeseburgers from Sam's Warehouse. I had to go down into a ditch about four feet below the road in order to feed them. I tossed the burgers to them and backed away. One by one, they inched forward and ate. Although I had placed myself in a precarious position, I knew instinctively and could feel in my heart that there was no danger from these souls.

When I returned home that evening, I sent out dozens of e-mails to local authorities and rescue organizations begging for help to capture the dogs. I knew that if I couldn't get assistance soon, my efforts would be in vain.

Two days passed, and I received only one response from my e-mails. Dennis McCullough with Hillsborough County Animal Services in Tampa offered to help. While I waited for Dennis, I spent three more long days returning twice a day to feed the dogs, each time gaining a little more of their trust. On the fifth day, Dennis, along with several others, traveled to the area while I was at work. He called me later to say he had successfully darted two of the dogs, knocking them out, and had them in his care. However, he hadn't been able to catch one and left her behind.

For the rest of that day, I wasn't able to get that poor remaining dog off my mind. The thought of her now alone in that horrible area wore heavily on my heart. I knew I had to go back there to find her and somehow get her to safety.

I found her lying in a ditch, waiting for her family to return. I called my husband, Art, who immediately came to my aid with a rope. I approached her slowly, holding the rope behind my back and extending my other hand with a cheeseburger. There was no fear. She instinctively knew that she was being saved and allowed me to put the rope over her head. Tears streamed down my face as I led her to the car, where she allowed Art to hug and pat her.

From that moment, she became our Heidi. She was clearly a sensitive and gentle girl. As we treated her for heartworms and other parasites that infested her body, she became healthier. And with each day, she became closer to my family: my husband, my mother, my son, my daughter, and Cassie, our yellow Labrador–Pit Bull mix, who adored her. But more than anyone, she bonded with me. Everywhere I went, Heidi's loving and gentle spirit was by my side.

Three months after rescuing Heidi, I found out I had lung cancer for the second time in my life. I was operated on, and the cancer was removed. After returning from the hospital, I was moved to a low-lying single bed in the living room, where I could watch TV and be with the family. Heidi chose to be by my side twenty-four hours a day, seven days a week. She made sure we were always connected, with either her chin resting on my stomach or her paw touching a part of me. When I got up to go to the bathroom, she followed me and waited outside the door until I came out. Then she walked beside me, carefully guiding me as I unsteadily made my way back to the bed. As I recuperated, it became increasingly evident that she sensed when I needed something and would literally retrieve a family member to come to me, even before I verbalized any need. She seemed to know when my pain medications were due or if I was having more pain than I could comfortably handle. It was as though she could read my mind. Her love was unlike any I have ever known.

It was hard having cancer for a second time. Heidi gave me a purpose to pull through. She needed me. At the time, I didn't realize that I was the one who needed her. I have no doubt Heidi saved my life.

Twenty-two weeks from the day I first saw Heidi on that desolate road, everything changed. The night of September 10, 2001, the evening before the horrible September 11 terrorist attacks on the United States, Heidi died suddenly of an aneurism, a blood clot that went to her brain and killed her instantly.

I truly believe that Heidi was an angel sent to me when I needed her most. Once her job was done and I was fully recovered, she was called upon where she was needed, to help guide souls to cross over that next morning. For five and a half months, I was graced to have Heidi in my life, a visiting angel who, in saving her life, saved mine in return.

Heidi's Legacy Dog Rescue
heidislegacydogrescue.com

Bonny

Red Dog Farm Animal Rescue Network
reddogfarm.com

"I could hear them squeal
with delight"

Donna Myers

My Jack Russell, Bonny, came to me after a friend went through a divorce and said she could no longer keep her dogs. I thought Bonny was adorable and offered to take her in. I had only had her for seven months when I noticed she was a bit standoffish around children, so I never pressured her to play with them. Because she looked like the dog "Wishbone" on TV, kids were always eager to meet her. But she kept her distance.

Bonny and I had a morning and evening ritual, playing fetch in a grassy area behind our apartment complex. Morning fetch time was around 7:15, which gave us a good fifteen-minute workout before I left for work. Evening fetch time was immediately upon my arrival back to the apartment at 5:15. Bonny was a good girl, never getting into trouble. She stayed home alone throughout the day, but she was ready to get out and play as soon as I walked through the door.

Playing fetch was something Bonny and I did alone. Or at least I thought we were alone. One of the apartment units backed up onto our favorite patch of grass. One day, I noticed two boys, about six and eight years old, pressed up to the window of the apartment, watching Bonny catch fly balls. Through the glass, I could hear them squeal with delight each time she leaped into the air to catch the tennis ball.

From that day forward, our sessions of playing fetch had an enthusiastic audience. The ritual went on for months, until one morning, I noticed the older boy was watching us from the sidewalk instead of inside his apartment. I assumed he was waiting for the school bus. Cautious because of Bonny's reservations about kids, I decided it was time for her to meet one of her biggest fans.

As we walked over to meet the boy, he ran away from us toward a small truck, opened the door, and revealed his little brother inside. The child, obviously paralyzed, was strapped in. At first sight of Bonny, his little body lurched forward, his face beaming. I brought Bonny up close, and the older boy picked up the limp hand of his little brother and gently stroked Bonny's head. I can't describe the look of joy on both of those kids' faces. Suddenly, Bonny raised herself up and licked the little boy on the cheek, then leaned toward his big brother and licked the hand that was holding up his little brother's hand to pet her. The boys let out a simultaneous "Aww." We left. They waved. I cried. Dogs know.

You never know the hurt that others endure in this world behind the closed windows of their lives, or the joy a simple act of kindness can bring.

Forgiveness

Acceptance Without Judgment

ChickPea

Dogs' Refuge Home
dogshome.org.au

I once had a relationship with a murderer. William Andrews tortured five people and was convicted for his part in the murders of three. When I met him, he'd been on death row in Utah for fourteen years and had never spoken publicly about the crimes. I was the corrections reporter for a television station and was determined to get an interview before his execution.

In an attempt to gain Andrews's trust, I visited him on death row every two weeks over a period of eight months. And I succeeded. Although I knew the horrific details of his crimes, I saw his humanity, and it scared me. It provided a truth that's hard to comprehend: bad people are capable of doing good things, and good people are capable of doing bad things. During the interview, Andrews asked his victims to forgive him. I didn't know how they could.

For most of my life, I've had a hard time grasping the concept of forgiveness. Why should people forgive? Religious texts say it's because God forgives us, so we should forgive others. Put into a spiritual context, it's about freeing yourself from the suffering caused by anger and hurt. It's not necessarily about letting the perpetrator off the hook. Still, for most people, finding forgiveness isn't easy.

Dogs, on the other hand, have a unique ability to forgive. They don't forget. When they have to, they tolerate. But most often, they forgive.

Since I was a child, I've felt empathy for dogs and other animals. I've rarely felt the same level of caring about people. There's a reason for that. Dogs have never let me down. People have. I hadn't given my attitude much thought until one day when I experienced a monumental epiphany.

It was 2007, and I was the president of one of the largest dog shelters in Australia. The Dogs' Refuge Home is a no-kill shelter that houses up to one hundred seventy dogs. At the time, it was a seventy-two-year-old nonprofit organization led by a committee, twenty-two staff, and one hundred active volunteers. The organization received no government funding and operated from money raised from boarding and pound facilities, a crematorium, and gifts from dog-loving human beings.

Anyone involved in charity work will tell you it's a labor of love. When you're involved in a charity that involves animals, it's complicated. Passion rules. Often, common sense does not.

Three volunteers were causing absolute chaos at the refuge. They yelled at staff, filed constant complaints, ignored health and sanitation guidelines, and even tried to discredit the organization with the press. In truth, they were three major pains in my ass, and they were killing the morale of the staff and other volunteers.

Every day, the majority of us were trying to raise the million dollars necessary to operate for a year and to provide a safe and loving environment for the dogs in our care. The other three were making sure we couldn't succeed. It wasn't enough that we had to witness the atrocities perpetrated against the innocent dogs by cruel members of society, but we had to deal with people issues, too. No one was moving forward.

It was the night before a staff meeting, and I was at my wit's end. The staff wanted answers. They wanted something done. The solution wasn't clear to me. How could I lead my team when I was unraveling along with them? Left with no other options, I asked for divine guidance.

I woke up the next morning, and my path was clear. I walked into the meeting confidently. I listened as the staff aired their complaints about the volunteers in question, and then I went out on a limb. I suggested that perhaps the volunteers identified with dogs and not people for a very important reason. Perhaps in their past, they had suffered at the hands of a human being and could only find solace from dogs. I asked if we might look at them as broken people, like some of the dogs that came to us, the "biters," lashing out after years of abuse. I looked around and noticed that many of the staff had tears streaming down their cheeks. Some were nodding. It was a moment that stood still. I hadn't fully understood it until it came out of my mouth. The truth was, most of us had empathy for abandoned and abused animals for a reason: we identified with them.

In the spirit of dog forgiveness and understanding, the troublesome volunteers were asked to leave our organization and to continue their good work where they were happier. Peace came upon us, and a valuable lesson was learned.

There's often a reason people and dogs bite. It's about self-protection. If we respect what we may not know about the suffering of others and look at them compassionately, we open the door that can lead to understanding.

Dogs, for a reason that can only be described as divine, have the ability to forgive, let go of the past, and live each day joyously. It's something the rest of us strive for. The truth is, if you respect what you don't know and live your life assuming that there are legitimate reasons why some people bite, you won't take it personally. The end result is the ability to find joy in your own life.

Angel and Stephenie

Bernese Mountain Dog Rescue
bmdrescueca.org

"It's easier not to respond to those who attack you"

Stephenie Hendricks

I had a rough beginning. My parents had a tough breakup that started before I was born and lasted until I was fifteen years old. Life was chaotic, sometimes violent. My father was mainly absent. My mother attempted suicide. After a series of small moves, I left my parents when I was sixteen to live with older sisters.

There was one constant in my life: my dogs. My father grew up surrounded by dogs. His father had run a sled-dog cargo business in Alaska. I believe Dad knew that animals were loyal and dependable from his own experience in his young life. When things got out of control in ours, he made sure I had dogs.

My dogs were my companions, but they also took care of me. I had a Saint Bernard named Gulliver who functioned as a nanny, and Lilliput, a Peekapoo (Pekingese-Poodle mix) who slept with me and even rode on the back of my pony with me. We were inseparable. Gulliver and Lilliput were the team who took care of me when I was young.

Years passed, and I never forgot the important role dogs had played in my young life. I was married and had two young daughters when I was introduced to a Bernese Mountain Dog at the girls' school. When that dog looked at me with its jaunty Maurice Chevalier smile, I was instantly smitten with the breed. It has been said that they cast spells, and that is what it felt like! Shortly thereafter, we had Angel.

Angel was dignified, wise, devoted, and deeply loving. She understood us and loved us all unconditionally. She was also a life coach.

For much of my career, I had worked as a television and radio talk-show producer in an environment of very competitive and brutal personalities who seemed to take pleasure in bringing others down, including me. With the influence of Jerry Springer on how talk shows were produced, I was being asked to do things that would hurt people's lives as a form of entertainment. The work environment was hostile. I chose to work less in order to have time to raise my daughters, which also gave me time to go on walks with Angel.

One day, Angel and I were walking on a beautiful trail, when two Jack Russell Terriers rushed us and attacked her. They barked and growled and then jumped up and bit into her, one hanging from each jowl. She held her head high, with the Terriers dangling off the ground, and looked at me as if to say, "If I do not acknowledge them, they will cease to exist." I implored her to shake them off her face. I was afraid of being bitten if I tried to grab them. But she remained impassive. They soon lost interest, dropped to the ground, and ran off. Angel's eyes looked deeply into mine, saying, "See? It's easier not to respond to those who attack you."

As we walked down the trail, I thought about Angel's message:

Don't engage. It takes your involvement to make a fight, and if you don't fight back when attacked, the fight doesn't really exist.

This was particularly pertinent to my gradual retirement from the tabloid talk-show environment.

I am much more grounded now. I've learned that provocative situations can be empowering and that I can avert destructive experiences, even when dealing with hostile people.

Years have passed, Angel is gone, but I'll never forget the gifts she gave me as a life coach. My experiences with her reinforced my observations that humans are low on the evolutionary scale of loving beings. As one of my daughters once mused, "Angel was very Buddhistic!"

"Cruelty can destroy the body but not the soul"

Vivian Axmacher

It was an early September morning just before dawn when a good Samaritan on her way to work found a tiny, matted, and emaciated dog. The dog was taken to a nearby shelter. He weighed three pounds, was covered in dried feces, and had little hair on his body. A veterinarian checked him over. He was filled with infection. Every tooth in his mouth was rotten, and the smell on his breath was of death.

Days passed. No one claimed him. No one missed him. It was clear that someone had dumped him. Being an animal control officer myself, I have seen many horrors associated with the abuse of cats and dogs. When I saw this dog at the shelter, I immediately knew he had been discarded from a puppy mill. He was a longhaired Chihuahua mix. I figured he was thirteen or fourteen years old and had served his purpose of siring as many puppies as possible. When I met him, he hadn't eaten in four days and was very ill.

The shelter volunteers called him UgMug, perhaps because his life had robbed him of his cuteness. When they took him outside on the grass, I watched as he pranced here and there, seemingly unaware that he was dying. I decided on the spot that I was going to foster and adopt this little guy and do my best to give him what he truly deserved, a chance to live.

It was a chain of events that ultimately played a role in saving the life of the dog I quickly named Mr. Handsome. After bringing him home, I hand-fed him anytime I thought I could interest him in the tiniest bit of food. But his mouth was so full of infection he wouldn't eat. Three days later, he took a turn for the worse, and I rushed him to the emergency vet. I walked into the office, and the first thing the vet said was, "I can smell an infection from here." I had only begun to tell his story when she asked if she could adopt him. She said that she and her partner would take care of his teeth in exchange for the adoption.

My heart sank, because I'd already fallen in love with the little guy. But I also knew that if he was going to get the help he needed, the operation that might save his life, I would have to let him go. And so I did.

Arrangements were made, and Mr. Handsome was soon a resident at the vet's office. Within days, he had undergone surgery. All but his bottom canines were removed, and he was neutered. He would spend the next three weeks recuperating from his ordeal, and we all kept our fingers crossed that he'd survive.

I called often to check on his progress. Although I knew he was in good hands, my heart still had a ping for the little fellow. Perhaps it was luck or destiny that three weeks later, the vet told me she could no longer keep Mr. Handsome. She said he required more time and attention then she could give. She asked if I would like him back. My heart jumped for joy.

Once he was at home with me, the challenge was to help him eat. His spirit was willing, but his gums were sore. I sat on the floor every day and night, testing different foods. The counter was lined with open cans and pouches of different dog foods, pieces of roast chicken, and thinly sliced steak. I cooked, chopped, blended, and mashed all of his food in a desperate attempt to give him nourishment. Most of the time, he would try a tablespoon and then walk away. But one day, everything changed.

I was eating my morning muffin, a butter rum muffin, to be exact, when Mr. Handsome became very excited about what I was putting in my mouth. From that day forward, the eating and healing began.

His preferred foods now are his daily muffin top, home-roasted chicken, and pork tenderloin. He has gained two and a half pounds,

Mr. Handsome

Bangor Humane Society
bangorhumane.org

his gums are healed, and his hair has grown back. He has returned my love and compassion with tiny licks and a bushy tail that wags when he greets me.

Mr. Handsome tolerated daily abuse and neglect. Oh, how he must have suffered with a mouthful of infected teeth. This was his life for thirteen or fourteen years, nearly all his life. I know that God touched my life through this little dog, creating a bond between us, a divine intervention to heal a tiny body with a beautiful soul. For this, I am grateful.

I have learned a lot from Mr. Handsome. He has reminded me of the evil in some and the goodness in others. He has shown me that cruelty can destroy the body but not the soul. He has taught me that when life seems difficult and the pain is more than I think I can bear, if I just believe in life and what I deserve from it, if I just keep wagging my tail, everything will be all right.

"My self-loathing disappeared"

Nancy Kaiser

My twenty-nine-year relationship with my husband was over. My soul mate, a yellow Labrador Retriever named Shadow, had died five months before. And now I was sitting on the vet's floor, crying and stroking the head of his brother Licorice, shattered by another painful good-bye.

I was learning to live without a husband, but I knew I'd never survive without Labradors to take care of me. Shortly after Licorice passed, Hana and Saba came to me when I needed love and support the most.

The puppies came from a breeder in Bedford, Virginia, and were pure joy. But within a week of them coming home, I developed flu-like symptoms and became very sick. Caring for and housebreaking the pups became infinitely more difficult, especially in the summer rains of North Carolina.

Hana was quick with his outside chores. Saba, the problem child, loved water but hated rain. Sick as a dog (no pun intended), I'd stand there with stubborn Saba sitting under my umbrella. Out-waiting him required strength and patience, two qualities my ill health stole from me.

One afternoon, after standing in the rain for too long, I lost it, and my anger erupted. I picked Saba up, shouted angrily at him, and stormed into the house. He looked up at me with adoring eyes, questioning my startling outburst. Instantly, I felt immense remorse and shame. I was overwhelmed with guilt. There was simply no excuse for losing my temper with him. At ten weeks old, Saba was too young to understand. Even though my unresolved anger toward my ex had contributed to my emotional meltdown, my temper tantrum was simply inexcusable.

Hana and Saba

Noah's Wish
noahswish.org

I was still berating myself an hour later, when tiny, sweet Saba plopped down on my foot. His gentle touch and selfless act of forgiveness initiated a catharsis. This little creature who forgave my indiscretion so quickly melted my heart. Saba's gesture freed me to forgive myself for my outburst and removed the shroud of negativity that engulfed me. My two-year inability to forgive disappeared with that one act of unconditional love.

As I got stronger and healthier, our training became easier and more fun. I learned far more from the little Labs than I taught. Hana and Saba were learning simple commands: sit, stay, down, come. While they mastered not peeing in the house, I learned to trust again, to love unconditionally, and my most challenging lesson, to forgive and let go.

Saba and Hana's happiness, joyful exuberance, and life-loving nature have provided powerful lessons for the woman who'd misplaced those childlike traits long ago. Because of them, I feel worthy of being loved, I'm able to give love without the fear of being hurt, I have forgiven my ex, and most important, I now love myself.

Animals live fully in the moment; they let go of their past and don't drag it around with them. This is one of the greatest lessons they offer humans. The universe sent Hana and Saba to teach me about true forgiveness. Both of them are master teachers. All of our pets are.

"It was a scary and unexpected afternoon"

Katherine Haloburdo

It's always a proud day for my black Cocker Spaniel–Poodle, Quincy, when we visit the special education class at our local elementary school. Freshly bathed and brushed, Quincy looks handsome in his shiny black curls and red collar. His fat paws lift with purpose, and his swagger turns to a trot. He happily passes classrooms heading for the door he knows is his.

Quincy marches into the classroom with the sides of his mouth turned up into an actual smile, his knobby tail wagging with delight. The students are waiting for him, sitting in a tight circle with the staff. All eight children have special needs, with severe physical and mental handicaps. All of them are excited to touch, smell, hug, and kiss the warm love known as Quincy.

Quincy walks around the room, allowing each child to say hello in his or her own unique way. Sarah wobbles left, then right. Her braces make it difficult to stand, but she manages, much to the delight of everyone. Sarah uses sign language to ask Quincy to roll over, and he does. Tony is autistic, and when he smiles, he lights up the room. He always asks Quincy for a high-five and gets it. Jake, who for our first year and a half sat at the back of the classroom for Quincy's entire visit, now sits within the circle and asks Quincy to do tricks for him. The response always solicits laughter from this very special group of girls and boys.

You might not expect this behavior if you knew Quincy's history. Quincy was taken from a house after neighbors complained of excessive barking. He had been kept in a small crate twenty-four hours a day, cramped, malnourished, uncared for. He was placed in a local shelter in Lancaster, Pennsylvania, and that is where we found each other.

I realized very quickly that despite a dreadful beginning, he exuded joyfulness and love and was extraordinary. I took him to several classes to learn manners and then to be certified as a therapy dog.

One day, as we visited our special class, Quincy was tested, and I was challenged. As usual, Quincy marched around the circle, saying his hello to all of the children. Before he reached one of the boys, he stopped, looked up at me, and refused to move forward. This was unlike Quincy; he had never acted this way before. I decided not to force the issue. Slowly, Quincy approached the boy, but he quickly backed away and let out a short, guttural bark. He had never barked in a classroom before. A moment later, Quincy moved forward, and the boy reached out to him. And then, without any notice, the boy went into a seizure, and the hand that had reached out for Quincy was now clenching his furry ear, pulling at it uncontrollably. The staff tried to unclench his fist, but they couldn't.

Quincy looked at me for reassurance. The only thing I could say was, "It's okay. It will be over soon." The seizure continued for what seemed like an hour. In reality, it was only a minute. In that minute, Quincy was as quiet as could be, his eyes telling me that he understood the boy didn't mean to hurt him. He didn't nip, didn't reach, he simply allowed the seizure to take its course and trusted that the little clenched fist would release.

When the boy's fist did release, Quincy did something that amazed me. He sat on his hind legs, placed his paws on the little boy's knees, and stood up and licked his face.

Katie and Quincy

Puppies Behind Bars
puppiesbehindbars.com

On the ride home from school that day, Quincy zonked out in the passenger seat, snoring the entire length of the ride home. I stroked his furry ear and acknowledged his fearlessness, tolerance, trust, and compassion for a little boy whose life is full of seizures. I honored his willingness to stay and not run. I was thankful for his trust in me that all would be okay.

Whenever I need reminding of what it means to be human, I recall that afternoon. I imagine that if everyone had the tolerance and forgiveness of Quincy, we would all smile more, trust more, forgive more, and most important, love more.

"She forgave our species for the sins of one"

Vivian Jamieson

My life is about animals. This is not a conscious choice but just the way I arrived on the planet. At the tender age of five, I started a horse club with my friends. For years, we ate, slept, and breathed everything equine. This wouldn't seem odd, except that growing up in the far reaches of northern Canada, we had never actually seen a live horse.

Today I'm a practicing veterinary specialist in ophthalmology, a passionate wildlife advocate, and the "mother" of three lovely dogs. Animals figure into every aspect of what I do. The grace of their constant company has influenced my attitude toward life. Don't sweat the small stuff, forgive and forget, and when given the chance, always eat—all valuable lessons gleaned from my furry friends. But there was one dear patient who taught me the greatest lesson of all, a lesson that has profoundly influenced the person I am today. Let me tell you the story of Phoenix.

I was finishing up my weekly appointments at a satellite veterinary office in Myrtle Beach, South Carolina, when I was asked by the emergency-clinic veterinarian to consult on the eye problems of a dog that had been admitted the night before. I sensed from him that this was not a routine consultation, but nothing in my twenty-five years of veterinary medicine could have prepared me for the heart-wrenching sight that was waiting in the next room.

The acrid odor of burned flesh assaulted my nostrils before I had rounded the corner. Instinctively, I pinched my nostrils. After being directed toward the appropriate cage, the smell increasing on approach, I knelt down and peered through the bars. In the back corner, barely breathing, lay a charred lump curled up on a plastic surgical drape.

I opened the cage door slowly so as not to disturb. The poor creature weakly raised its head toward me. Gazing into the disfigured face caused me to wince. Could this be a dog? Two eyes bugged out like huge headlights on a chassis of scorched skin, because there were no eyelids to cover them. "It is better if she comes out on her own," Sue Anne, the veterinary technician, said. "Come on, sweetie, we won't hurt you," she cooed.

After painfully struggling to her feet, the poor thing limped out of the cage. Only then did I realize that 75 percent of her body was suffering from second- and third-degree burns. "What happened?" I asked Sue Anne, knowing that only a house fire or perhaps a fiery car crash could have accounted for such devastating injuries. I feared for this poor dog's owners. A nudge to my right leg caused me to glance down. In spite of the obvious pain, the scorched puppy had hobbled over to tap me with the raw tip of her nose. Relaying her desire for affection, her singed tail wagged ever so slightly.

I leaned down to pet her but hesitated when I realized that every part of her body was scorched and painful. There was nowhere to lay a comforting hand. My heart sank. "She's an eight-month-old Pit Bull, and last night, her thirteen-year-old owner decided to throw gasoline on her and set her on fire," Sue Anne told me with disgust. "Neighbors saw him do it and ran over to save the dog, but . . ." The young girl's voice trailed off, overcome by emotion. "I'm afraid she may be beyond saving."

I felt another nudge on my leg as the disfigured puppy persevered for my attention. Kneeling, I tickled the tip of her nose, the only thing I could think to do. She nuzzled in beside me, wincing each time her damaged tail wagged. She was unable to contain her joy at the affection, perhaps the first real affection of her short life. "It's never too late to try," I said, wiping the tears as they collected in the corners of my eyes. I was suddenly filled with determination to win the fight for this sweet dog's life. "Let's get started with some lubrication for those eyes."

That night, on the ride back to the main clinic in Charleston, the loving little dog was in my thoughts. Were we really doing the right thing by prolonging her suffering, when her chances of survival were remote and the road to recovery so painfully long? Perhaps we should put her out of her misery. I was thankful that in veterinary medicine, we had the option for a tragedy like this one. But there was no denying the Pit Bull's spirit. She wanted to live. You could feel her will when you looked beyond her horrendous injuries and into her trusting eyes. Perhaps for now, we should take it one day at a time.

And what of the boy who had tried to kill his own pet? I could not fathom what had happened in his young life to elicit such violence. His ruthless actions toward something so defenseless represented the worst of the human race. What had we humans created in this boy, and what was to be done with such cruelty? And yet the Pit Bull, when betrayed so viciously by her human master, responded with the quiet faith that different humans would not hurt her but rather would help relieve her agony. She didn't lump us all together but somehow trusted that there was kindness and compassion in others. She forgave our species for the sins of one, not letting such cruelty replace her joyful trust with fear or retaliation.

Phoenix, as our disfigured friend came to be known, was soon transferred to our veterinary specialty practice in Charleston, where a team of volunteer veterinarians, technicians, and others began the arduous task of piecing the dog back together. Months of skin-grafting surgeries and physiotherapy followed. It took five hours of delicate ophthalmic surgery to rebuild her eyelids so her vision could be saved.

Through the months of painful recovery, Phoenix's patient and loving spirit never wavered. In time, we all fell in love with her. Eventually, when we could bear to part with her, a loving family adopted Phoenix to enjoy life at home—to romp in a backyard, to sleep at the end of a bed, and to beg for table scraps. The last time I saw her, although she was still sporting a T-shirt to protect her sensitive hairless skin from the sun, Phoenix was as good as new and as playful as ever.

As for her young offender, the delinquent youth was convicted of animal cruelty and was sentenced to several years in a youth facility. I hope he is getting the help he desperately needs. I venture to say that Phoenix would want it that way.

Since that fateful day when I stared into the eyes of a severely burned puppy and saw love where there should have been loathing, or at the very least fear, I have not been the same. When my mind clouds with petty grudges or minor grievances or when I am pulled down by life's struggles, I have only to think of Phoenix and her forgiving ways to redirect my steps back to the high road. This one special dog taught me that with so much joy in the world, it's a shame to waste time on anything else.

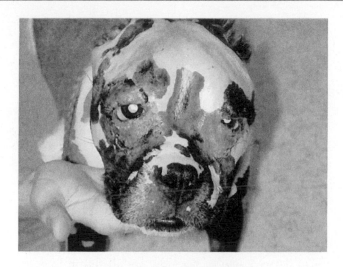

Phoenix

Vision for Animals Foundation
visionforanimals.org

ChickPea and CousCous

Afterword

During the past sixteen years, I've made my own family with one man and two dogs. It's been filled with love, laughter, and joy. These have been the best years of my life.

The day I signed with a publisher to write this book, I asked my girls, CousCous and ChickPea, to write it with me. I knew it was a hard ask. They were both old and feeling it. Cous could barely walk, and Chick was having seizures that were coming more often. Our time was limited, but I knew they'd stay if they could.

The day after I finished this book, in what I can only describe as a divine exclamation point, my darling ChickPea was beamed up to a joyfully euphoric place after passing away from a suspected brain tumor.

I'd like to share her story, because she may have taught me the greatest lesson of all.

It was just before Christmas, 2001, and I had a strong feeling that someone at the Dogs' Refuge Home (where I volunteered) needed me. I walked in and asked if we had a really needy dog. The answer was no. So I walked out through the gate, heading toward my car. One of the staff ran after me. "We do! We've got a really sick dog. She's too sick to be adopted. She needs her eye out. We haven't raised the money yet to get her fixed up."

"That's who I'm here to see," I said. "Show me the way."

I followed the girl to a dark section of quarantine kennels not seen by the public. She opened a kennel door, and out sauntered Lizzy, an overgrown and badly matted Shih Tzu. She looked up at me with an eye that showed mainly only the white. Her cornea was lost somewhere under the lower lid. I smiled. At that moment, in that dark kennel, it was as if the sun had broken through on a cloudy day. I scooped her up and whisked her away, promising to love and foster her.

She was so imperfect, but she was perfect—for me. I walked through the door of the house with my new bundle and set her down in front of my husband. He looked at the hairy mess looking up at him with one wonky eye and firmly announced, "That is the ugliest dog I've ever seen. I don't want that dog in my house, Jenny!"

"We're fostering her," I said. "She's sick. We're going to help her through her eye surgery."

"We're not keeping that dog, Jenny . . ." His words trailed as I walked away.

CousCous, my darling, sweet Maltese-Pomeranian, echoed Jon's thoughts with her eyes. She would put up with this dog but only temporarily.

Lizzy, whom I promptly renamed ChickPea, was suffering from two eye infections, a urinary tract infection, skin disease, ear mites, and two deformed and strangely twisted front legs. Her toenails had grown into circles from not being clipped, and she was badly matted. She was a mess—my mess.

I administered antibiotics and slathered on ointments and creams, determined to get her to good health. There were many trips to the veterinarian and the veterinary ophthalmologist. Infections cleared, and ChickPea's bad eye was removed. She didn't appreciate it. She sat outside in the garden, looking longingly to escape through the gate. At mealtime, she had knock-down, drag-out fights with CousCous over food. I didn't know much about her, but I did know that she wasn't grateful for the rescue. As much love as I poured into her, it wasn't returned. If I sat down on the couch and started to pet her, she'd jump off. The only place she seemed to find solace was at Jon's feet.

When ChickPea was recovered, I took both dogs to the groomer. They each had a puppy cut and came out looking like sisters from the same litter. Jon couldn't believe it. "You've transformed her, Jenny! It's amazing," he said. I immediately thought to myself, "She's in!" But Jon's demeanor quickly changed from doting husband to parental father.

"Follow through, Jenny. Follow through."

"What are you talking about?" I asked.

"You said she was a foster. It's time to take her back."

"But she likes it here," I said.

Jon spanned the room with his arms. My eyes followed, ending with the French doors looking out onto the bay scattered with sailboats. "Who wouldn't like it here?" he exclaimed.

"Fine. I'll call the refuge today. She's up for adoption."

As I walked out the door to attend a daylong retreat, I glanced into the TV room. Jon was on the couch, bookended by two fluffy white dogs. One hand was resting on ChickPea, stroking her gently.

I returned late that afternoon and was greeted by the two dogs at the door. ChickPea had a ribbon around her neck. "So, she got a home?" I asked.

"Yes, she's got a home," he barked. "Call that dog refuge and tell them to stop calling here!"

Apparently, over the course of the day, the refuge had called three separate times, saying they had interest in the one-eyed Shih

Tzu. Jon saw the light and decided she belonged right where she was.

Days turned into months. We noticed that the better Chick-Pea felt, the funnier she became. ChickPea was a comedian. She made it her job to entertain us. She took great pleasure in making us laugh. We started playing the "I'm going to get you" game. I'd say, "I'm going to get you," and she'd cock her head, smile, and take off, running between couches and chairs from room to room as I chased her, often colliding with a piece of furniture, crying out, and then getting right back to the game. There were no disabilities in her world—she took her situation as it was and chose to enjoy all she had.

Jon preferred to take his morning walks with ChickPea. And when he visited his dad in the afternoons, he took ChickPea. A quick trip to town—ChickPea. The two had found each other. She was like Jon. She loved cautiously. She didn't hand you her paw or lick you affectionately. Instead, a real treat came when she jumped up on the couch and decided to sit next to you instead of on the other end.

Try as we could to heal ChickPea's body, her health issues continued. There were eye operations, daily eye drops, and monthly visits to the ophthalmologist to save the existing eye. There were chronic urinary tract issues and skin issues and monthly antibiotic injections to treat the unending infections that raged inside her. She battled on without complaint.

On her good days, she chose to be with Jon. When she didn't feel well, she came to me.

Over the years, her hearing disappeared, and the vision in her remaining eye became limited, like seeing movement through a milky fog bank. She took it all in stride, relishing rides in the convertible, runs on the beach where the sand promised her freedom, and her nightly spoonful or two of vanilla ice cream. But more than anything, she loved CousCous, whom she relied on for sight and hearing and whom she truly adored.

On that last day, Jon chose to hold her in his arms. We were all brave for the veterinarian who came to our home. Afterward, as we sat huddled around our beautiful one-eyed girl, CousCous rested her head on top of ChickPea's, and we all let out a collective sigh of loss. "Our girl is gone, Jenny," Jon cried. "She taught me more about life than any person ever did."

Fourteen days later, CousCous was very sick. Jon was in New York, and I was in Australia. I told him I was on my way to the vet. When I spoke to him again an hour later, I was holding her in my arms. He asked how she was. "She's gone." I sobbed. "Our baby is gone."

Jon let out a cry that I felt on the other side of the world. And as I held my girl and cried on the phone with my husband, it all became clear. He felt the same way I did. It wasn't just me. He felt it, too. They were our kids, our family, and our gifts. Because of them, we were better people.

I've learned a lot about life from unexpected teachers. Jon taught me about humanity. From CousCous, I learned how to be joyful. And ChickPea, the lion in my Oz, taught me about courage. She showed me how to live life in spite of my past and left me with a motto that I call hers: Even when there's quite a lot wrong, you can still enjoy what's right.

May the lessons you've learned in this book help carry you through life, and may you always know the divinity of dogs.

Acknowledgments

The beat of my heart has been shared with Clara, Sally, Fluffy (the cat who acted like a dog), Petey, Clemmie, Whitney, Paget, Mary, Philophal, NickDingo, Sadie, Gigi, Emily, Locumia, Frodo Frog, Honey, CousCous, and ChickPea. My love for these souls surpasses words.

My sun shines when I'm around animals and the people dedicated to helping them. I'm grateful to everyone who rescues and whose heart is filled with empathy for others. In my lifetime, I've been involved with organizations whose members have become family. I love this family and admire and respect all of its warriors.

There is a peace within me because of my sister Kate, who has been a beacon of light throughout my life. Her compassion is contagious, and her dedication to the voiceless is admirable. She's my hero. I also give thanks to my mother and father for teaching, by example, love for all souls.

There is a skip in my step because of my literary agent, Susan Raihofer, and her continued confidence in my abilities. We never have a meeting in which laughter is not involved. I'm blessed to have her represent me, and I'm grateful to the late Abner Stein, who, with clear precision, clasped our hands together. Simon & Schuster's Atria Books editor Sarah Durand fought for the right to work on this book. I love that and her peaceful presence in my work. Jess Loo provided giggles, foster dogs, and technical know-how during this process. She also comforted me when I cried. I love you, Jess.

I have continued hope in humanity because of the people I'm lucky enough to call friends. You know who you are! I thank you for your love and support.

If there's a storm that rages inside me, it's because of the fact that we have to battle the limitless greed that motivates some to abuse and exploit animals. Unless we join forces against puppy factories/mills, our work will never end. When you buy a dog and cannot physically see where it came from or meet its parents, there's a very good chance that you have just paid someone to abuse another dog. Caged like factory hens and often diseased, matted, and malnourished, these dogs are purposely hidden away so people can't see how they're treated. Unless we work on laws that put an end to puppy factories and do not participate in buying dogs that come from these people, the horrific abuses will continue. Please join in the effort to end the cycle. I thank all of you who are already doing your part, and I share your pain.

The gifts I've been given are many and include the contributors who divinely found their way into the pages of this book. I thank them for sharing their very personal stories and for taking this journey with me.

The song in my heart has been provided by every dog I've had the privilege of knowing. Thank you, my divine friends, for showing me the way.

Contributor Index

Photography Credits

In order of appearance: William Skiff, Darwin Ender at Darwin Ender's Photography, Camille Boisvert, Harry Bandy, Andy Buckley, Jeanne Bowen, Jennifer Skiff, Glen Bradburry, Deb Lander, Beth Lockhart, Jeff Gosselin, Michael Thompson, Susan Hartzler, Jennifer Skiff, Susan Lilly, Jessica Clark, Judie Tardiff, Debi Boies, Doug Bauman, Glenwood McNabb, Bruce Skakle, Jennifer Skiff, Patty Howe, Lauretta R. Allen, Robert P. Baker, Marilyn Tyma, Carol Bradshaw, Kathy Klingaman, Ann Forrest, DeVeau Sleeper, Jennifer Skiff, Eduardo Gaitan, Andy Keye at Whitney Photography, Michele Newman-Gehrum, Cheryl Denis, Dorothy Lemme, Avery Gagnon, Matthew Talbot, Sandra Church, Deana Whitfield, Jennifer Skiff, Stefan Gahlin, Sheri Soltes, Tonya Werner, Jim Fernald, Steve Parr, Linda Schroeder, Troy Wells, Tom Sullivan, Elaine Smothers, Jane Caruso-Dahms at Contemporary Concepts Photography, Linda Pugh, Genie Gardipee, Barbara Keyser Grice, Julie Hawkins, Alex Cearns at Houndstooth Studio, Kelly Hendricks, Vivian Axmacher, Nancy A. Kaiser, Robert Grossman, Heidi White, Alex Cearns at Houndstooth Studio.

About the Author

Jennifer Skiff is an award-winning journalist, television producer, and author. Her #1 inspirational bestseller, *God Stories: Inspiring Encounters with the Divine*, is published in seven languages.

For more than a decade, Jennifer traveled the world working as an investigative environmental correspondent for CNN. Her programs promoting animal welfare have aired on The Discovery Channel and networks globally. Among other honors, she's received the prized Environmental Media Award.

Passionate about animals and their welfare, Jennifer works with charities throughout the world to bring relief to abused and abandoned animals. She is a trustee of the Dogs' Refuge Home in Australia and is a director of the SPCA HC and Pilots N Paws in the United States.

With her favorite Aussie and beloved dogs, Jennifer spends her life in perpetual summer between Maine and Australia.

jenniferskiff.com

Look for the musical companion to this book, *The Divinity of Dogs: Music to Calm Dogs and the People Who Love Them*, on iTunes and Amazon. The pieces were coproduced by Jennifer Skiff with composer and pianist George Skaroulis. The author gifts 25 percent of after-tax profits from this book to charities of her choice that legislate against animal abuse and promote sterilization.